The Science Writers' Investigative Reporting Handbook

A Beginner's Guide to Investigations

LIZA GROSS

Watchdog Press
KENSINGTON, CALIFORNIA

Published by Watchdog Press, Kensington, California.

Book Layout ©2017 BookDesignTemplates.com
Cover design by Liza Gross. Detail from GFP-labeled Drosophila multidendritic sensory neurons, copyright CC BY-SA 2.0, flickr, balapagos.

This project was funded in part by the National Association of Science Writers Peggy Girshman Idea Grant. The views and opinions expressed in this handbook do not necessarily reflect those of the National Association of Science Writers.

The Science Writers' Investigative Reporting Handbook/ Liza Gross. — 1st ed.
ISBN-13: 978-1-7323339-0-1 (paperback)
ISBN-13: 978-1-7323339-1-8 (e-book)

Contents

Dedicated to fearless reporters everywhere,
and the loved ones who support them.

"On my best days, I feel I am directly involved in a vital dialogue with the American people, telling them truths they need to know for our democracy to work. Without facts, deception will win. Free people need a free press."

–Jane Mayer

"Truth is always tentative, always has room for sharpening and improvement."

–Philip Meyer

Foreword

"THE SCIENCE WRITERS' INVESTIGATIVE Reporting Handbook" is the third in a series of how-to guides produced by members of SciLance, a community made up mostly of independent science writers and journalists. The first book in the series, "The Science Writers' Handbook: Everything You Need to Know to Pitch, Publish, and Prosper in the Digital Age," outlines the critical skills required to master the craft and business of freelance science writing. The second, "The Science Writers' Essay Handbook," lays out the art and elements of writing and publishing powerful essays.

This book offers an introduction to investigative reporting for anyone who's thought about launching an investigation but isn't sure how to start. It explains what investigative reporting is, and what it isn't, by reviewing some of the fundamental principles of investigative reporting. It makes the investigative strategies, tools and methods accessible to anyone hoping to add accountability reporting to their stories. You'll learn what investigative reporters mean by a "documents state of mind," and find tips on choosing an investigation, tracking down sources, organizing materials and interviewing subjects. This book is not intended to serve as an exhaustive resource on investigative journalism (though you'll find such materials in Chapter 7, "Funding, Resources and Further Reading") but to introduce you to the tools, approaches and mindset that investigative reporters use.

Many science journalists likely have an affinity for investigative reporting without realizing it. Good science journalists, like good investigative reporters, have highly developed analytical skills, unbridled curiosity, a healthy skepticism and a knack for sussing out dubious claims. And there are clear parallels between the methods of science and those of investigative reporting. Scientists and investigative reporters test hypotheses about how the world works, though investigative reporters typically do so with an eye toward revealing situations where things aren't working as they should. Investigative reporters, like scientists, gather data to test their hypotheses, and consider alternative explanations for the patterns that emerge. They start with a premise — sometimes following a tip or a hunch — and then search for information that can help them test the veracity of that premise as well as key assumptions that arise over the course of reporting. Information might come from dusty old documents, computer databases or people, some helpful, others hostile. A good investigative reporter, like a good scientist, never discounts evidence that disproves her hypothesis.

This book will give you the confidence and guidance to start digging beneath the surface to uncover bias, hidden influence and flaws in science-related endeavors or simply to bolster the evidentiary foundation of your stories. The materials presented in this book are suitable for students, science journalists of all kinds and anyone interested in the pursuit of truth. And though a good investigative reporter nurses a healthy sense of outrage, in this age of "fake news" and "alternative facts," anyone who cares about science and evidence-based policies will benefit from adopting the tools and mindset of an investigative reporter.

At its essence, investigative reporting, like all good reporting, gives citizens the information they need to make rational decisions about matters that affect their lives. When I worked at the Exploratorium, San Francisco's storied science center, in the early 2000s, I experimented with ways to write about science to help people engage with the world around them. I remain inspired by the vision of its founder, Frank Oppenheimer, a particle physicist who, as part of his brother Robert's Manhattan Project, helped develop the atomic bomb. Oppenheimer founded the Exploratorium in part to help society keep in check the destructive power great scientific minds had unleashed. He believed that giving people the confidence and tools to understand scientific phenomena would help them become more engaged in the world, and perhaps even capable of holding those great minds to account. "If we stop trying to understand things," Oppenheimer once wrote, "I think we're all sunk."

Science writers with the confidence and tools to dig beneath the surface of their stories can serve a similar purpose. Democracy depends on an informed and engaged electorate, which must increasingly grapple with complex scientific issues. Science writers can and should tell stories that reveal a deeper sense of the truth about the scientific enterprise and scrutinize the institutions that use and produce science. In doing so, they will give readers not only the information they need to understand science in public debates but also the tools they need to participate in debates about science that affects their lives.

The federal government spends billions of dollars on scientific research each year — under the assumption that basic research and the fruits of that research advance the public interest — while billionaires increasingly bankroll science based on their own interests. Reporters who follow the money — and treat science as a human endeavor like any other — will inform citizens when research is serving the public interest and when it's serving the interests of powerful people and corporations. With apologies to Margaret Mead, never underestimate what one person committed to pursuing facts that powerful interests want hidden can reveal.

[1]

What's Investigative Reporting Got to Do With It?

THE PRIMARY DUTY OF ANY REPORTER, investigative or not, is to find and tell the truth. We seek the truth by obtaining information from a wide range of sources. We interview people, confirm or reject the veracity of their claims, mine facts from documents, correspondence, data and archival material. Over the course of reporting on a complex issue, we may gather a massive amount of material, which we then organize, analyze, interpret and verify to arrive at a defensible account of what we've discovered.

Some believe that all good journalism is investigative journalism. Among them is Carl Bernstein, whose legendary reporting with Bob Woodward on the cover-up of the Watergate break-in precipitated President Richard Nixon's downfall. "I'm not one who really believes that there's a pseudoscience called investigative journalism that's different from all the rest of journalism," he told the online outlet Big Think [1]. "I think all good reporting is the same thing — the best obtainable version of the truth."

Surely any serious science reporter aspires to tell true stories. We aim to illuminate issues that affect people's lives or influence society at large. We tell readers things they don't know to help them make sense of the world around them. We gather information from multiple sources, and verify its accuracy, to the best of our ability, in order to tell the truth as we found it. We investigate topics thoroughly so we can write about them with authority. Does that mean we're doing investigative journalism?

Political reporters like Bernstein come from a tradition that views journalism as an independent monitor of power. They embody the adage "Journalism is printing what someone else does not want printed; everything else is public relations." (Though the saying is often attributed to George Orwell, there seem to be no original documents to confirm that he said it. That's why investigative reporters like to repeat the old saw "If your mother says she loves you, check it out.") And that style of journalism, it turns out, is very much in keeping with the Cambridge Dictionary definition of investigative journalism: "a type of journalism that tries to discover information of public interest that someone is trying to hide."

Many science writers, by contrast, come from a tradition that values the ability to translate esoteric scientific concepts into accessible language. Some came to the profession as scientists who realized they'd rather write about science than do it. Some gravitated to the field to cover the frontiers of knowledge. Others wanted to tell stories about the process of discovery. For many, writing about science has little to do with holding powerful interests accountable or printing what someone doesn't want printed.

Science writers tend to be "into science" and explaining things, says veteran investigative reporter (and my mentor) Joe

Bergantino, and may not appreciate how much more work it takes to uncover rather than simply explain something. "A lot of people just don't get that," he says.

Far too often science journalists are trained to think that the official version of an event, the principal investigator's version, is the truth, says Deborah Blum, who directs the Knight Science Journalism Program at the Massachusetts Institute of Technology, where she teaches investigative science journalism. "I think a lot of people come into science journalism thinking that's the story they're going to tell," Blum says. "That they're going to illuminate the experiment. They're going to listen to the PI and try to explain his or her perspective."

Yet one of the most important things journalists do is recognize that the official version of any story is only one part of the truth, Blum says. The truth is multifaceted and, in the end, science is really just about people trying to understand the world around them. "That doesn't elevate it from being a human enterprise just like everything else, full of hubris and ego and mistakes and cover-ups and all the other things that attend to every human enterprise," she says. "And we cheat ourselves, we cheat our readers, we cheat the public and frankly we cheat the community of science itself when we don't cover it that way."

While investigative stories often expose abuses of power and corruption among captains of industry and politicians, power concentrates in the halls of science just as it does in the halls of commerce and government. Scientists may not wield power in the same way CEOs and politicians do, but they help shape technological trajectories, medical treatments, culture, business — the very fabric of society. Plus, a large share of science operates on the public dime, and scientists help decide what to fund. Taxpayers have a right to know how their money is spent, whether it goes to politicians, police or scientists.

Science writers can play an essential role in democracy by scrutinizing science as if it were any other enterprise. That means holding scientists and scientific institutions accountable, and giving citizens the information they need to understand when science is being abused or manipulated for personal, political or economic gain. It also means not accepting anything at face value — even if the information comes from someone who holds a Nobel Prize.

Investigative journalism is a pillar of democracy, but it's also critical to the integrity of science, says Blum. "Everyone needs a watchdog."

It's easy to get caught up in the wow and wonder of science, she says, and there's a place for those kinds of stories. "But I think if we look at the way science journalism works, that can only be part of it."

A major reason science journalism doesn't include more investigations is the time and effort involved, says veteran investigative reporter Charles Piller. "There's just a lot less of it done, because most publications don't have the budget for it," explains Piller, who writes for Science magazine.

News about developments in science and explanatory journalism about the majesty and wonder of the natural world are important topics and of great interest to the public, he says. "However, they're really just part of the story about this human endeavor and how it should be interpreted by the public. That's why investigations into all the elements that might undermine or corrupt or influence the way in which scientific work is understood and interpreted are really vital."

And the need for science-savvy journalists who can monitor and scrutinize all the ways science is used and abused has arguably never been greater.

Every administration politicizes science to some degree. But the administration of President Donald Trump has dismissed science in pervasive and, in some cases, unprecedented ways. "From Day 1, the White House and its lackeys in certain federal agencies have been waging what amounts to a war on science, appointing people with few scientific credentials to key positions, defunding programs that could lead to a cleaner and safer environment and a healthier population, and, most ominously, censoring scientific inquiry that could inform the public and government policy," The New York Times editorial board wrote in the fall of 2017 [2].

Trump left the majority of top science positions vacant for his first year in office and filled others with corporate allies who have attacked environmental, health and safety rules on behalf of regulated industries. His appointees, many of whom have long denied the threat of global warming and humanity's role in driving it, have ordered the words "climate change" removed from government websites. Top-level science advisers at the Environmental Protection Agency now include a who's who of industry-friendly scientists who have denied the health risks of well-known toxic chemicals and air pollutants, including flame retardants, asbestos and ground-level ozone. And in an unprecedented move, EPA Administrator Scott Pruitt barred scientists who receive EPA grants from serving on agency advisory panels, arguing that the funding would cloud their objectivity. Many of the scientists are leading university researchers who once offered independent advice on EPA regulatory concerns, including environmental toxicology and air pollution. Pruitt replaced these academic researchers with a group that included industry-funded scientists and state officials with a history of opposing federal regulations.

Against this backdrop, public mistrust of science is increasing, exacerbated by reports of scientific misconduct, retractions in biomedical and psychological research and undisclosed conflicts of interest that help corporations manipulate science. We know now, thanks to scholarly studies and investigations by journalists, that the tobacco, chemical, pharmaceutical, sugar and food industries have financed research to deny, obscure or cast doubt on evidence that their products cause harm [3, 4, 5, 6]. These manipulations have clouded the scientific consensus on technical issues, making it hard to tell whether sharp divisions of expert opinion are real or manufactured.

Complicating matters, social media platforms have facilitated the rapid, widespread distribution of misinformation, hoaxes and conspiracy theories that are difficult to dispel once unleashed, even when there is no evidence to support them. Baseless theories are even harder to combat when they involve issues that evoke strong emotional responses, with vaccines, gun violence, evolution and vaping being prime examples.

Scientists create their own credibility problem when they say, "Trust us, we're the experts," and project an air of authority that is beyond their expertise, Piller says. As examples, he points to issues associated with research, such as the safety of scientific experimentation and risks and rewards associated with a project. "These are issues that often the general public has opinions about and might have views that are equally or even more relevant than what scientists think," he says. "Investigations can kind of intercede and shed light on those cultural, social and political issues that are often addressed very incompletely or sometimes even in an arrogant way in the scientific community."

The products of scientific discovery can have far-reaching impacts on the general public and shape the way people live. Yet in a growing list of cases — cloning, the creation of artificial life forms, de-extinction, geoengineering, brain-to-brain interfaces

— there is no direct mechanism for the public to shape the trajectory of these fields or the ethical and regulatory frameworks that govern them.

Cultivating an informed electorate requires reporters who can navigate this complex terrain. Science journalists are well equipped to sort through these issues, bring emerging ethical and regulatory issues to light and counter false claims, whether promoted by politicians, corporate interests, free-market absolutists or scientists. And they have an important role to play in monitoring who wins and who loses as scientists deploy emerging technologies in a lightly regulated landscape.

Good science journalists already give readers the facts and the context to make sense of those facts. But we can also dig beneath the surface to learn the story behind the story, and discover what or who is behind false claims. This might mean sniffing out evidence of powerful interests bankrolling misinformation campaigns or outfits pushing dodgy claims for political, economic, ideological or personal advantage. It might mean revealing that a leading fossil fuel company hid its own scientists' evidence about the dangers of global warming while leading a campaign to deny climate change science [7]. Or it might mean showing that the chemical industry spent millions of dollars to block legislation that would keep flame retardants in consumer products while hiding evidence of their harm [8].

By digging beneath the surface, science journalists can determine when society's ability to address pressing problems is compromised by individuals or organizations that distort scientific evidence to advance their own interests. In an age when climate deniers and creationists can reach the highest elected offices in the land, the challenge isn't finding examples of people in power abusing science — it's deciding which abuses to investigate.

References

1. Interviewed by David Hirschman, "Big Think Interview with Carl Bernstein," July 22, 2010. http://bigthink.com/videos/big-think-interview-with-carl-bernstein
2. The Editorial Board, "President Trump's War on Science," New York Times, Sept. 9, 2017. https://www.nytimes.com/2017/09/09/opinion/sunday/trump-epa-pruitt-science.html
3. Lisa A. Bero, "Tobacco Industry Manipulation of Research," Public Health Rep, March-April 2005; 120(2): 200–208. doi: 10.1177/003335490512000215. https://www.ncbi.nlm.nih.gov/pmc/articles/PMC1497700/pdf/15842123.pdf
4. Frederick S. vom Saal and Claude Hughes, "An Extensive New Literature Concerning Low-Dose Effects of Bisphenol A Shows the Need for a New Risk Assessment," Environ Health Perspect, Aug. 2005; 113(8): 926–933. doi: 10.1289/ehp.7713. https://www.ncbi.nlm.nih.gov/pmc/articles/PMC1280330/
5. Adriane Fugh-Berman, "How Basic Scientists Help the Pharmaceutical Industry Market Drugs," PLoS Biol, 2013; 11(11): e1001716. https://doi.org/10.1371/journal.pbio.1001716
6. Maira Bes-Rastrollo, Matthias B. Schulze, et al., "Financial Conflicts of Interest and Reporting Bias Regarding the Association between Sugar-Sweetened Beverages and Weight Gain: A Systematic Review of Systematic Reviews," PLoS Med, 2013; 10(12): e1001578.

https://doi.org/10.1371/journal.pmed.1001578

7. Neela Banerjee, Lisa Song and David Hasemyer, "Exxon: The Road Not Taken," InsideClimate News, Sept. 16, 2015. https://insideclimatenews.org/content/Exxon-The-Road-Not-Taken
8. Liza Gross, "Money to Burn," East Bay Express, Nov. 11, 2011. https://www.eastbayexpress.com/oakland/money-to-burn/Content?oid=3042155

END NOTES

- ✓ Investigative reporting takes far more time and effort than explanatory reporting, but it is a pillar of democracy and critical to the integrity of science.
- ✓ One of the most important things journalists can do is recognize that the truth is multi-faceted: the official version of any story is only one part of the truth.
- ✓ Taxpayers have a right to know how their money is spent, whether it goes to politicians, police, regulators or scientists.
- ✓ Science journalists can play an essential role in democracy by scrutinizing science as they would any other enterprise.

[2]

Investigative Reporting Essentials

GETTING AT THE TRUTH can be hard enough when you're telling stories about complex science. Explanatory science stories can involve weeks of research and field reporting to capture the nuances of an experimental setup or months of intensive study to limn the edges of scientific knowledge. Gathering, analyzing and turning all that material into a compelling narrative requires focused curiosity, discipline and obsessive attention to detail. Yet there are differences in degree and kind between even the most in-depth explanatory science stories and investigative reporting.

Notwithstanding the objections of reporters who topple presidents, it's useful to consider how most definitions of investigative reporting distinguish it from other forms of journalism. The nonprofit Investigative Reporters and Editors (www.ire.org) defines investigative journalism as "reporting, through one's own initiative and work product, matters of importance to readers, viewers or listeners. In many cases, the subjects of the reporting wish the matters under scrutiny to remain undisclosed."

A variation on that definition, which comes from UNESCO's

"Story-Based Inquiry" [1], includes matters that aren't purposefully hidden: "Investigative journalism involves exposing to the public matters that are concealed — either deliberately by someone in a position of power, or accidentally, behind a chaotic mass of facts and circumstances that obscure understanding. It requires using both secret and open sources and documents."

At a 2013 meeting to explore models of muckraking around the world, Global Investigative Journalism Network Executive Director David Kaplan described investigative journalism as "systemic, in-depth, original research and reporting." Quick-hit scoops based on a leaked document aren't investigative reporting, Kaplan said, though they could point the way to an investigation.

A science journalist might use a document from a source to report that a scientist fabricated data, for example, and that's an important story. But a truly investigative science story, by Kaplan's and others' definition, would present original findings based on the reporter's own in-depth research and analysis. This might involve a survey of several years of a scientist's work to see if the fabrication was part of a pattern and to identify potential factors behind it.

Veteran investigative reporter Joe Bergantino uses a pithy definition in his trainings: "Investigative reporting is making something public that someone would rather keep secret that's of public importance."

Bergantino, who co-founded and now advises the New England Center for Investigative Reporting, broke the story about James Porter, a priest who had sexually assaulted dozens of children in the 1960s while the Catholic Church turned a blind eye. Hundreds of victims of sexual abuse at the hands of priests filed suit against the Boston Archdiocese after Bergantino's story, which led to Porter's conviction. Only a decade after Bergantino's 1992 investigation for Boston's WBZ-TV did the Boston Globe's Spotlight team reveal the extent of sexual abuse in the church, and its efforts to shelter the abusers.

DISTANCE FROM SOURCES

The movie "Spotlight" came out in 2015. Terry Ann Knopf, prompted by the film, wrote in the Columbia Journalism Review that until Bergantino broke the Porter pedophilia case, Boston reporters had failed to cover the Catholic Church in the same way they covered government, business and other institutions [2]. Bergantino agreed with Knopf's assessment a few weeks later in the Huffington Post (now HuffPost) [3], noting that for many Boston reporters, "reverence and respect for the Catholic religion — in many cases, the religion of their childhood — blinded them to possible wrongdoing inside the institution itself."

The Porter story "unleashed a torrent" of local and national coverage of the issue that lasted through the late 1990s, Bergantino wrote, when reporters believed there wasn't much more to cover. But then Boston Phoenix journalist Kristen Lombardi reported that church leaders knew about the abuse in 2001, the same year editor Marty Baron brought an outsider's perspective to the Boston Globe. Baron fought to unseal court documents and devoted the resources and reporters necessary to connect the dots and blow the story wide open.

Soon after Bergantino's story paved the way for a new era of church coverage, investigative reporter John Crewdson charged science writers with being far too close to their subjects to recognize conflict and corruption when they see it. Science journalists like science and they want their readers to like it too, Crewdson, then at the Chicago Tribune, argued in a 1993 piece called "Perky Cheerleaders."

They're excited by the prospect that the scientist they're covering has discovered something big [4], he wrote. "So they just ask him how to spell whatever it is and write it down."

While the best stories a general reporter can get are the ones the politicians and bureaucrats don't want them to have, Crewdson continued, "the best stories a science reporter can get are the ones somebody wants to put out."

Even then, though, some were digging deeper. Since the early 1970s, Daniel Greenberg had been scrutinizing big science as a form of government spending like any other in his newsletter, Science and Government Report. (Greenberg has also characterized the science section of newspapers and trade journals as a "cheering section.") The year before Crewdson's critique, MIT's Blum had won the Pulitzer Prize for a series published in the Sacramento Bee that examined ethical issues in primate research. That same year, Robert Capers and Eric Lipton won a Pulitzer for a Hartford Courant series that showed how a flawed mirror crippled the Hubble Space Telescope [5].

Still, tropes about science reporters as stenographers have continued to crop up over the years, as seen in a 2016 Pacific Standard article [6]. "There's probably no field of journalism that's less skeptical, less critical, less given to investigative work, and less independent of its sources than science reporting," freelance journalist Michael Schulson wrote.

A damning indictment, if true. But does the evidence support it? I agree that science needs more investigations — that is, after all, the point of this handbook. But there are many good reporters and outlets covering science and scientists with a skeptical eye, starting with Buzzfeed's ongoing coverage of sexual harassment in science. (For other examples, see Chapter 4, Finding Investigative Stories.) And even Science magazine, which depends on an audience of scientists for subscriptions, announced a new fund for investigative reporting in 2017.

Yet Schulson's point remains: Independence from sources is

critical for investigative reporting — along with a simmering outrage at injustice.

CULTIVATED OUTRAGE

Stories that expose priest pedophilia, serial sexual harassers or decades of deceit in the fossil fuel industry are prime examples of what it means to reveal matters of public importance that someone would rather keep secret. They're also good examples of why investigative reporting is sometimes called the journalism of outrage. It's no accident the acronym for Investigative Reporters and Editors is IRE.

That sense of outrage leads to one of the most critical differences between explanatory and investigative reporting: intent. Investigative reporting seeks not merely to inform but to *re*form, to expose injustice, wrongdoing, abuse of power. How does that differ from activism, you might ask? And how can you be objective if you set out to identify social problems that need fixing?

Objectivity has long been a beacon for best journalism practices, but the term is slippery. In "The New Precision Journalism," Philip Meyer, professor emeritus and former holder of the Knight Chair in Journalism at the University of North Carolina at Chapel Hill, says the tradition of objectivity was intended to keep journalists from imposing their own viewpoints on readers [7]. But this model, he argues, was "designed for a simpler world, one where unadorned facts can speak for themselves."

Letting facts speak for themselves was arguably never a good strategy for reporting on science, which can require considerable context to understand. And today, with scientific output doubling every nine years or so, it can be dangerous, especially when journalists give unsupported hypotheses published in the literature the same credibility as facts or well-tested theories. Consider what happened after the now-defunct journal Medical Hypotheses published a speculative theory that mercury in vaccines causes autism. News stories repeated the notion as "one side of a debate" without noting that no credible evidence supported it — or that the journal trafficked, in its own words, in "*probably untrue papers.*" For years, reporting on vaccines as well as climate change slavishly followed a "he said, she said" model of quoting anti-vaccination fanatics and global warming deniers, ostensibly to appear objective. Instead, the stories produced false equivalence, helping to fuel confusion and controversy on issues where the science was settled.

Many journalism critics, including Dan Gillmor, have argued that invoking objectivity to mean "free of bias" has created more confusion than clarity. We're all human, with our own opinions, points of view and competing interests. And try though we might, we can't just check a lifetime's worth of baggage at the door when we show up to work. We can, however, adopt processes, just as scientists do, to keep those biases from tainting the accuracy of our work. Gillmor has suggested ditching the idea of objectivity and focusing instead on the principles it was meant to embody: thoroughness, accuracy, fairness and transparency.

By embracing these principles, you can develop a process that helps you form and test hypotheses and gather and evaluate information while keeping your biases at arm's length. The process should be robust enough that if someone else were to reproduce your investigation, following the same procedures, they'd arrive at the same conclusions. (See Chapter 5 for more on testing and verifying hypotheses.)

Bracing for Backlash

There's a good chance that the conclusions of an investigation born of outrage will trigger backlash from the subjects of your investigation. Explanatory stories are more likely to paint subjects in a good light, leaving their reputations intact, even boosted. Investigative stories, by contrast, can undermine the reputations and authority of established scientists and science institutions.

Exposing something that someone is trying to hide requires courage. Powerful people and those with a stake in an issue you're reporting on are more likely to have the inclination and means to retaliate, even if you've gotten it right. And you should be prepared for backlash.

When I revealed hidden interests behind debates about the risks and benefits of vaping for The Verge in 2017 [8], the Twitter trolls came out in force with attacks on my story and credibilty. To maintain my sanity, I turned off my Twitter notifications for people I didn't follow. And though I was well aware that online bullying and intimidation are part of vaping advocates' strategy to silence critics, it was still a bit unnerving. I took some comfort in knowing that it was important to inform the public about tobacco companies' role in sowing doubt and discord, and tried to ignore it as best as I could.

Getting attacked and even getting threats are part of the job, says Science's Charles Piller. "If you want to do this work, that's part of it. It's very satisfying to be able to have beneficial effects on society associated with digging deeply into something ... but you have to be willing to have sleepless nights and to have a thick skin and to be willing to piss off a lot of people."

The best way to prepare for backlash is to make sure your story is rock solid. Good investigative reporting, like good science, is built on a defensible, meticulous, transparent foundation. That means relying on primary sources such as government and court documents, eyewitnesses, audio and visual recordings and archival texts. It also means not just collecting facts but subjecting them to a rigorous verification process and substantiating them in a way that can be replicated.

HIGHER BURDEN OF PROOF

Challenging authority or revealing wrongdoing requires a much higher burden of proof than explanatory reporting because the stakes are higher — for both subject and reporter. There's an extra layer of responsibility that comes with producing news based on your own research, rather than simply reporting someone else's findings. The evidence needed to make the case that a scientist has committed fraud, or that a self-described "sound science" group actually distorts science to defend industry interests, far exceeds that needed to explain how Arctic terns manage an improbable 44,000-mile round trip from pole to pole each year or to describe the latest efforts to unlock the mysteries of dark matter. As important as such stories may be, they're unlikely to put you in legal jeopardy.

"Fact-checking is certainly important in all reporting, but it becomes extremely important in investigative reporting, given that you're usually saying something negative about somebody or some company," Bergantino says. "You've got to get your facts right and make every effort to get the other side, far beyond what you would normally do, because of the nature of the material."

With investigative science journalism, it's not unusual for matters of public importance to be concealed behind a mountain of difficult to decipher technical information. You may need to find experts who can help you interpret data or documents correctly. But the essential approach to getting the facts right is similar for any investigation and depends on taking a systematic and intensive approach to reporting: interviewing multiple sources (including, of course, the subjects of the investigation), compiling a trove of documents that corroborates information you've gathered or, just as important, suggests caveats or qualifications that you should acknowledge.

To get the evidence you need for a story, you may need to obtain databases or build your own. Critically, you should create a reporting diary that allows you to retrace the steps you've taken to arrive at your conclusions (see Chapter 5 for more on reporting diaries). This is especially important because the truth you find typically arises not from any one piece of information but from a pattern of facts that emerges slowly over time through careful analysis. You might think there's no way you'll forget how you arrived at a particular conclusion, but it's best not to take that chance.

Because investigations can be so time-consuming, investigative reporters often spend a lot of time up front deciding what to cover, to ensure that all the investigative work is likely to pay off.

These added layers of time and effort are essential because failing to nail down an investigative story carries the potential to cause harm. When you allege wrongdoing or abuse, you have to make sure that you've ruled out alternative explanations for what you've found, that others can replicate any data analysis involved and that you can defend not just the facts you've gathered but also the logic behind your interpretation of the facts.

Allegation versus Investigation

Without documents to substantiate charges of wrongdoing or impropriety, what you have is not an investigative story but an allegation-and-denial story. Such stories report allegations and often give the accused parties plenty of space to respond, thereby minimizing the grounds for libel. Investigative reporting goes beyond "he said, she said" stories to excavate the evidence needed to determine whether the allegations are grounded in facts.

Fairness and accuracy in reporting require that you give any subject of an investigation the chance to offer their side of the story. Depending on the story, you may want to do this as early as possible, in case there's an innocent explanation for what you think you've found. (For more on when to confront subjects, see Chapter

3.) Even if your subject fails to deny or adequately explain what you've found, that's no guarantee they won't try to discredit you or your reporting when the story comes out.

Any reporting errors leave you open to attack, and even minor mistakes can undercut and distract from your central findings. If you get details about an experiment wrong, you run a correction. If you get details about an allegation wrong, you may get sued.

Consider what happened when The Times of London suggested in a trio of articles that several anti-smoking experts were on the payroll of Big Tobacco.

The October 2016 stories reported that Britain's largest cancer charity had "condemned" a group of academics "central to the debate on e-cigarettes in Britain" for taking large sums from tobacco companies, implying that their funding had influenced their views on e-cigarettes' safety. There was also a sidebar that listed four experts under the headline "Academics Making a Packet" (British for "making a bundle"). Although the articles said the scientists had declared their competing interests as appropriate, they did not provide evidence to substantiate claims that the scientists took tobacco industry money or that doing so compromised their work.

Soon after the stories ran, the paper issued a correction and an apology to one of the experts accused in the story, Clive Bates, for suggesting he was "making a packet" from tobacco companies: "We accept that Mr. Bates paid his own travel and accommodation costs and does not receive any funding from tobacco or other nicotine companies." Several weeks later, after the other experts named in the story threatened to sue The Times in an article in a competing newspaper [9], The Times retracted the stories and issued a full apology: "The experts mentioned in our report ... are internationally respected for their longstanding global work to reduce smoking, and their work on the issue of nicotine harm reduction. Our report and a panel headed 'Academics making a packet' implied that these experts had received funding for research into e-cigarettes. We accept that this was wrong and that their work has not been tainted by the influence of tobacco industry funding. We apologise for our errors and omissions and for the embarrassment caused."

The original story was removed from The Times' website, though enterprising reporters can find a copy at well-stocked libraries. The piece did imply that the experts named had taken tobacco money and that the industry funding had influenced their statements and research regarding the safety of e-cigarettes. What the piece did not do was provide independent evidence, such as invoices or industry contracts, to substantiate those claims. Instead, the story used innuendo and quotes from other experts to make its case. As a result, the piece simply presented allegations, without proof, which did not stand up to scrutiny.

The Times stories made serious charges against prominent experts that could damage their reputations and careers — exactly what the subjects claimed in threatening to sue the paper [10].

An investigative story can lay out allegations through third parties, but it has to provide corroborating evidence to back up the charges. In the case of allegations about scientists taking industry funding, this might come in the form of a research contract or grant, an internal company memo or a canceled check — all verified as authentic. Or it might come through analyzing the competing interest statements found in research papers or from background checks of researchers that reveal a pattern of undisclosed industry funding and conflicts of interest in studies that favor an industry product.

This type of evidence not only turns a "he said, she said" story into an investigative story but it adds a layer of transparency to the investigative reporting process by showing readers how you know what you're reporting. It adds a foundation of evidence that allows readers to decide about the validity of allegations for themselves. It also provides cover against legal action.

Instead of simply relaying unvetted allegations or reporting the latest research on e-cigarettes without noting the vested interests at play, an investigative story, or one that uses investigative tools, would dig beneath the surface to show readers the reality behind the appearances.

Sometimes reporters get tips about shady research practices or undisclosed industry affiliations. Information can originate with one source, but it can't end there. Even the most trusted sources can have a hidden agenda or personal reasons for pushing a particular narrative. And even sources who have a track record of providing reliable information can get things wrong. That's why single-source reporting is not investigative reporting. But just because different people tell you the same thing, that's no guarantee it's true either. They could be promoting the same agenda or have different reasons for saying the same thing. You have to figure out how your sources know that something is true, preferably with documents or other primary materials that support what they say.

I tend to be conservative on this question, but it should be noted that many of the stories that uncovered Watergate relied only on (anonymous) human sources, whom Woodward and Bernstein often described as "reliable sources." Some situations may call for a similar approach, especially if you have two or three independent sources giving you the same information and have exhausted avenues to find documentary evidence. But prudence dictates that you handle such stories with extreme caution, and discuss the pros and cons of using only human sources with your editor.

Every journalist strives to ensure what they're writing is true. But many science journalists are used to reporting the news, not making the news. It can be nerve-wracking to accuse a person or organization of doing something wrong based on your own reporting. When you uncover something that someone wants to keep hidden, based on your own initiative, you sweat the small stuff. You lose sleep. I've certainly spent nights before a story was about to run staring at the ceiling wondering if I'd overlooked something. That's why it's absolutely vital to continually question your hypotheses and assumptions as you gather new information. If something you uncover seems to cast doubt on your central hypothesis, keep digging until you can resolve a discrepancy or discover you were wrong and need to change course. And if something seems too good to be true, it probably is.

Telling the stories behind the stories is hard and time-consuming work. You have to do preliminary research before even launching an investigation, then you have to spend considerable time gathering the evidence needed to go beyond false balance and "he said, she said" stories. But all that effort can be immensely rewarding when you manage to affect people's lives for the better.

References

1. Mark Lee Hunter, et al., "Story-Based Inquiry. A Manual for Investigative Journalists," UNESCO, 2009. http://www.storybasedinquiry.com/
2. Terry Ann Knopf, "Where Were Boston's TV Stations During the Church Sex Abuse Scandal?" Columbia Journalism Review, Feb. 26, 2016. https://www.cjr.org/criticism/where_were_bostons_tv_stations_during_the_church_sex_abuse_scandal.php
3. Joe Bergantino, "Where Boston's TV Stations Were During the Church Sex Abuse Scandal," Huffington Post,

March 8, 2016.
https://www.huffingtonpost.com/joe-bergantino/where-bostons-tv-stations_b_9385624.html

4. John Crewdson, "Perky Cheerleaders," Nieman Reports, Winter, 1993.
http://1e9svy22oh333mryr83l4s02.wpengine.netdna-cdn.com/wp-content/uploads/2014/04/Winter-1993_150.pdf
5. 1992 Pulitzer Prizes.
http://www.pulitzer.org/prize-winners-by-year/1992
6. Michael Schulson, "How Journalists Can Help Hold Scientists Accountable," Pacific Standard, March 22, 2016.
https://psmag.com/environment/journalists-should-hold-scientists-accountable
7. Philip Meyer, "The New Precision Journalism," 1991.
https://www.unc.edu/~pmeyer/book/Chapter1.htm
8. Liza Gross, "Smoke Screen," The Verge, Nov. 16, 2017.
https://www.theverge.com/2017/11/16/ 16658358/vape-lobby-vaping-health-risks-nicotine-big-tobacco-marketing.
9. Alexandra Topping, "Anti-Smoking Experts to Sue Times for Claims of Tobacco Payouts," The Guardian, Oct. 23, 2016.
https://www.theguardian.com/media/2016/ oct/23/anti-smoking-experts-to-sue-times-for-claims-of-tobacco-payouts
10. "Top Scientists Hire Libel Lawyers to Sue Times," New Nicotine Alliance press release, Oct. 24, 2016.
https://nnalliance.org/activities/news/137-top-scientists-hire-libel-lawyers-to-sue-times

End Notes

- ✓ Investigative journalism involves exposing matters of public importance that are concealed — either deliberately, or accidentally, behind circumstances and facts that obscure understanding. It requires using both secret and open sources and documents.
- ✓ Quick-hit scoops based on leaked documents aren't investigative reporting, but could point the way to an investigation.
- ✓ Independence from sources is critical for investigative reporting, along with a simmering outrage at injustice.
- ✓ Following processes that ensure thoroughness, accuracy, fairness and transparency can keep your natural biases in check and help you defend your story against backlash.
- ✓ Investigative stories, which can damage reputations and livelihoods, require a higher burden of proof than explanatory stories.
- ✓ Create a reporting diary to make sure you can prove how you know what you reported.
- ✓ Nailing down every detail in an investigtion is essential because critics will use even minor mistakes to discredit the main premise of your story.
- ✓ Continually question your assumptions during the reporting process. If something seems too good to be true, it probably is.

[3]

Cultivating Sources: Documents, Data and People

INVESTIGATIVE REPORTERS OFTEN reconstruct events that we haven't witnessed firsthand, much as detectives do. We track down evidence from every conceivable source, follow paper trails, mine databases and interview people intent on hiding information. While there are many parallels between the methods of investigative reporting outlined below and those of police investigations, it's worth noting a key difference: police can legally lie to subjects to extract information, but journalists who make a habit of lying to sources will quickly run out of people willing to talk to them. (See Chapter 6 for a discussion of rare cases when deception may be warranted.)

Veteran investigative journalists talk about working from the outside in, through hierarchies of information to establish a pattern of events. This approach is usually rendered as concentric circles, with the outer ring representing secondary sources, the next primary documents, the inner ring representing human sources and your subject being the bull's-eye. (You've probably seen a version of this on TV, where detectives place the murder victim in the center of a big bulletin board and draw circles and lines leading to everyone connected to the deceased.) To guide your reporting, it can be helpful to draw the circles on a piece of paper or whiteboard with key sources in each ring as soon as you have an idea of what you're looking for.

You might draw a separate map of human sources, with spokes radiating out from your subject to potential sources in successive rings according to their proximity to the target. Think broadly about perspectives you might need, for example, from institutions (regulators, grant funders, hospitals), experts (scientists, lawyers, educators), activists and affected communities, and then identify people who might have useful information.

Veteran investigators also speak of a "documents state of mind" — meaning there's a fingerprint for everything — and a "data state of mind," in which you think about ways to quantify what happened: How often does something occur? How widespread is the problem? Data can also lend authority to a story, moving from anecdote to numbers that reveal systemic problems and hold those responsible accountable.

I took this approach for a story about violence at California's psychiatric hospitals [1]. After a patient strangled a psychiatric technician at one of the state's five hospitals, officials assured the public they'd taken measures to protect patients and staff. I asked a simple question: Did the rate of violent incidents go down in the years after the psych tech's death? Then I figured out what data or records I would need to answer the question and where I could find them. I ultimately obtained what I needed from multiple sources, some of which were available in online databases, while others required filing public records requests with the hospitals and other state agencies. The data showed the state's claims were false, and a hospital psychiatrist who was willing to talk to me made the data come alive.

Data and documents can help you uncover important stories about powerful people abusing the public trust, vulnerable people being harmed or corporations hiding incriminating studies.

Documents can also lead you to human sources who can help you interpret and vet the documents you have and find others you don't. The tips below will help you figure out how to find the information you need to tell compelling investigative stories.

COME UP WITH A REPORTING PLAN

Once you've done enough preliminary reporting to come up with your main question, create a plan to guide your reporting. Every investigation will follow its own path, but typically will require these basic elements:

- Identify documents and databases you may need and public records you'll have to request.
- Identify people you should talk to (based on expertise, role or affiliation).
- Figure out what places you may need to visit.
- Consider visual elements that can illustrate key ideas.

This list will invariably expand over the course of your investigation, but can help you organize the things you need to do. Keep the list close at hand, or on a whiteboard or Google doc (or whatever notetaking app you use) and then keep track of what you've done and what you still need to do.

REQUESTING PUBLIC DATA AND DOCUMENTS

Before you ask for data or documents from a government agency, get to know what's covered under the law. In addition to the federal Freedom of Information Act, or FOIA, each state has its own public records laws. Some information is exempt from records laws — in California this includes trade secrets, patient medical records and pending litigation — so there's no point in wasting time asking for them. Still, government officials have discretion over what they release, and you may need to negotiate to get what you want.

Numerous resources help journalists with public records requests (see Chapter 7 for more information), but it's important to keep a few things in mind. Many states have open records portals, but they typically offer a fraction of the materials the public has a right to inspect. For example, the Department of State Hospitals is part of California's open data portal, but includes just three datasets, a tiny portion of data collected, and presents only summary data of violent incidents. By poking around on agency websites you can find reports with graphs and tables that indicate the types of data that are collected. Ask for the underlying raw data, rather than settling for summary data, which might not provide the level of detail or context you need.

You might think government employees are trying to stall or put you off when they say they don't have what you're asking for. But Sarah Cohen, the former data editor of The New York Times and now Knight Chair in Data Journalism at Arizona State University's Walter Cronkite School of Journalism and Mass Communication, notes that employees often don't know what data their agency collects. You usually have to do a fair amount of reporting before you even ask for data so you can make your request as specific as possible. To figure out what data a government agency collects, ask for a copy of every blank form they have, Cohen advises. If necessary, find people at the agency who can tell you how the form is used, and whether it's part of a series of forms that paints a larger picture. That way, you can send in any relevant forms along with your data request to show them exactly what you need — and to show them that they do in fact collect it.

If you're trying to get documents from one of the many science agencies at the state or federal level and the people who work there can't or won't help you, check meeting minutes, audits of programs, inspector general reports, even footnotes. All can point you to documents or datasets that are produced in the course of government business.

Sometimes you can find government documents through more sophisticated Boolean searches that specify websites and file types, for example: glyphosate AND site:gov AND filetype:pdf. You can find spreadsheets by searching for filetype:xls.

In the digital age, a "documents state of mind" has expanded to include a "database state of mind," says Brant Houston, Knight Chair in Investigative and Enterprise Reporting at the University of Illinois and former executive director of IRE. What this means is that when someone tells you something, you find out if there's a document (or dataset) that supports or contradicts what they've said. People can change their stories easily, but it's very difficult for documents to change their stories, he says. "They're more like petrified information."

One document, or dataset, will often lead to other sources and questions that ultimately create a document trail. And if there's one thing all scientists and science organizations excel at, it's creating data and documents.

Just as an investigation should start with a specific question, it's a good idea to hunt for data that can answer a specific question. Move beyond trying to figure out what happened to thinking about ways to quantify what happened: How many times has a doctor taken payments from a drug company without declaring the funding on research papers? How much money has a climate change-denying politician taken from the fossil fuel industry? How much support has a nonprofit "pro-science" organization received from foundations with an anti-regulatory mission?

Keep in mind: state laws specifically say how much agencies can charge for things like copies, programming fees when necessary or discs. Know the law so you can contest overcharging or prohibitive fees intended to make you go away. Ask for electronic records to make it easier and cheaper for agencies to fill your request. This also allows you to easily search for keywords and saves you from having to create your own database from hard copies. You don't want to wait months for records only to receive PDFs of spreadsheets. There are tools to scrape data from PDFs, but why waste the time and effort?

Organizing documents

Organization is critical when you're gathering large volumes of documents. Thinking carefully up front about how to name and categorize documents will not only help you make sense of them, but will also help you retrieve specific bits of information easily when you need them. You'll likely want to create a system where documents appear in multiple categories to cover your bases. Depending on the volume of documents you've collected, it may help to create an index.

Valerie Brown, an independent journalist based in Oregon, always creates a timeline from documents as an organizing tool. She found this especially valuable for a story with Lizzie Grossman on how the chemical industry hired toxicology consultants to fight regulation [2]. "If you have various events like regulatory decisions, founding dates of industry consultancies, passage of relevant laws, environmental disasters, etcetera, it's very helpful to have them displayed all along the same track, because sometimes that reveals relationships you couldn't see before," Brown says. "For example, we could see in our article timeline that from the 1980s on there was a gradual increase in the number of consultancies in regulatory toxicology, in parallel with the attempts of the growing EPA to get a handle on chemicals and their toxicity."

Whiteboards also provide a visual reminder of the types of documents and data you have, and how they relate to each element of the story. If you were doing a story showing that an industry hid knowledge that their product caused harm, for example, you might use court documents (depositions, testimony and exhibits) to lay out historical context, while scientific papers might show the evolution of evidence in the field and whether industry-sponsored studies bucked the scientific consensus.

INTERVIEWING DATA

Treat data as you would any other source: figure out where it came from (if you didn't request it), and whether it's reliable. Even if it comes from a credible source it could still have problems. California's pesticide use database is the most comprehensive in the United States, but it's notoriously messy. Many fields are missing, incomplete or contain implausible values. Data entry is a tedious job, and people make mistakes.

Before you can figure out what needs to be cleaned up in a dataset, you have to know what's supposed to be there. Get to know the data starting with the record layout, or data dictionary, that lists the tables, fields and columns in a database. Table field headers are often in code, so you'll need a lookup table to understand what the fields are. Then you can scan the data for obvious problems. Ask experts who work with this type of data to spot check it for you, and to help you with the analysis later, if necessary. You may have to find other datasets to verify or cross-reference your data (for example, in the case of California pesticides, I knew that county agricultural commissioners also track pesticide use, and that data helped confirm the accuracy of my statistics).

Keep a data diary that logs everything you know about it (source, date acquired, date updated, etc.) and note any data processing or analysis steps. (See Chapter 5 for more on data and reporting logs.) Find reports that can serve as independent checks on the figures you come up with and that can flag discrepancies that might be mistakes or confirm that you're on the right track.

You might even discover the official numbers are wrong, which will strengthen your story. When you're ready to write a draft, see if you can come up with the same figures from scratch, without consulting your data diary. That way, you'll know not only that your analysis is sound but also that others will be able to replicate it if they choose to.

To learn more about how to use data in your reporting, consider enrolling in one of the regular boot camps offered by the National Institute of Computer-Assisted Reporting (see Chapter 7).

IDENTIFYING AND DEVELOPING HUMAN SOURCES

Data and documents may provide the foundation of an investigation, but we can't tell stories without people. Sources are more than our guides through thickets of complex science, datasets and documents. They also help us bring the documents and data to life, to show readers who is affected by the problems we unearth and why they should care.

Anytime you're trying to find information on an organization you suspect of shady practices, start by looking for "formers," ex-employees who may be willing to talk. People who no longer work for a company may not feel the same loyalty or obligation to an outfit as they did while on the payroll. They may finally feel free to speak about company dealings they long considered unethical or illegal. Even better, they may have access to confidential business information agreements, sealed court documents, internal company memos or other information that isn't publicly available. If someone offers you a tip, ask if they can help you document the information. It's important to recognize, however, that "formers" may harbor grudges, which can be double-edged: grudges can give people an incentive to speak with you but may compromise the quality of information provided. Their information may also be outdated, though it could provide important background or a line of inquiry you can follow up with others.

Since I report on the chemical and tobacco industries, I often scan business and trade newsletters to see who has retired, a habit I picked up after reading that the great investigative reporter Seymour Hersh found many of his CIA sources by following retirement announcements. You can also find retirees from specific companies through LinkedIn searches or by Googling "retired" and the company name. There's no guarantee they'll talk to you, but it's worth a shot.

If you're interested in investigating biotech or medical device companies, read trade newsletters and magazines to look for people who challenge the company line or offer a skeptical view of tests that promise more than they can likely deliver. It also pays to scan blogs and social media, especially Twitter, where people tend to sound off. If you find someone willing to talk with you, ask them to recommend other individuals to contact.

When you find a key source, do a background check. Come up with a routine that allows you to feel confident you've vetted sources. Do simple Google and social media searches, and check for criminal and civil convictions through PACER (Public Access to Court Electronic Records, an online database of records from federal appellate, district and bankruptcy courts), state courts and police blotters. You don't want to miss something that could undercut a source's credibility.

It can be difficult to find people who've been affected or victimized by the problems you've uncovered. Each story is different, but start by contacting organizations that might be able to identify potential sources. If you're writing about violence at psychiatric hospitals, for example, contact the nurses' union to see if they can put you in touch with someone willing to talk. If you're writing about neighborhoods dealing with toxic exposures, contact community health or activist organizations to find out if there are any meetings you can attend to talk with local residents. If you're writing about a medical condition, see if there's a support group on Facebook or some other social networking platform, and introduce yourself as a reporter who'd like to speak with someone about their experiences.

When a problem isn't recognized by officials, it can be hard to figure out who's most affected, as Climate Central reporter John Upton discovered. In an investigation based on research showing which communities faced growing flood risks from rising seas [3], Upton could see that Atlantic City stood out but the data didn't drill down into neighborhoods. "It took me a while to find the neighborhoods hardest hit by flooding, partly because nothing is being done to address the flooding there, so nobody official had any reason to want to talk about them," Upton says. "I drove around to all the flood-prone areas that experts and officials had told me about, but found that the impacts there were mostly to roadways — not so much to homes. Eventually, through word-of-mouth, social media and local journalists, I found working-class neighborhoods where residents routinely have to wear waders if they're going outside, and have to park their cars in other neighborhoods when storms coincide with high tides."

Upton also spent a lot of time in Atlantic City to get a feel for the culture and local economy. He hung out in casinos and neighborhoods, drank at local bars and eavesdropped on conversations to get a sense of what was on people's minds.

When approaching vulnerable people, transparency is critical. It's important to clearly state your reporting objective, especially for people with no media experience. You might suggest an introductory meeting so the person has a chance to get to know you before agreeing to an interview. It may take time to develop a relationship to the point where someone feels comfortable talking with you. Imagine how you'd feel sharing a traumatic event in your life with a stranger who asks you to relive the experience in excruciating detail. Explain what the potential consequences of going public with their story might be, and that you can't guarantee a given outcome.

Remember: no one has to talk to you. Your first obligation is to the reader, but sources who agree to speak with you — including subjects of your investigation — are critical to doing your job. Treat them with respect.

CONFIDENTIAL AND ANONYMOUS SOURCES

Using anonymous sources is tricky, especially for a freelancer. Most outlets have policies governing anonymity for people quoted in a story (for example, requiring that the information is confirmed through two independent sources) and often tell readers why a source was granted anonymity (a whistleblower could lose her job) to boost readers' trust. The Society of Professional Journalists offers this advice on anonymous sources: "Identify sources whenever feasible. The public is entitled to as much information as possible on sources' reliability. Always question sources' motives before promising anonymity. Clarify conditions attached to any promise made in exchange for information. Keep promises." (https://www.spj.org/ethics-papers-anonymity.asp.)

In some cases, confidential sources might provide tips or act as sounding boards, but are not quoted in a story. Either way, it's essential to have an explicit agreement up front regarding conditions of anonymity and how you'll use information provided. If you promise confidentiality and then reveal a source's identity, you not only risk losing credibility, you could also be liable for breach of contract. Make sure you determine who else knows the information your source is providing. You don't want to inadvertently reveal their identity by reporting information that could be traced back to them alone. Ensure that all information related to your source is securely stored.

Although journalism depends on the presumption of confidentiality between reporters and their sources, much like lawyer and client, there are no federal "shield laws" to protect journalists from being forced to reveal confidential information or sources in the United States. Close to 40 states now afford some measure of protection, but the parameters of that privilege vary. (See Chapter 7 to learn more.)

There's a difference between granting confidentiality to someone for an element of a story and hinging an entire investigation on a source who can't be named. Information from an unnamed whistleblower, for example, might help you get other people to speak on the record. Or an unnamed source might provide you with documents. But there are several things you need to consider when dealing with someone who will speak to you only off the record. Could the person have a motive to lie or mislead you? Might they have a grievance against the person they're accusing? Are they trying to float a theory to provoke a reaction?

Science's Charles Piller will rarely quote people who aren't named in a story, and then only when he has other sources and documents that validate what they say. "No story that I would ever write could be done exclusively based on people who can't be named," says Piller. "There has to be validation and documents and named sources. Some stories just can't be done because you can't get that."

Credibility, and discretion, in dealing with anonymous sources is a two-way street. You have to figure out whether their information is valid, and they have to have a reason to trust you. If someone's giving you background information that could be critical to developing a story but doesn't want their name in the story, they probably don't want you telling other people you're talking to them, either. "You can really harm people with these stories," Piller says. "You can cost people their jobs, cost people their livelihoods, careers can be damaged."

Piller builds trust with sources by telling them he's offered confidentiality to other people as well. "People understand that," he says, "and it has the advantage of reassuring them that you're being straight with them."

Even when someone is willing to be named, it's helpful to make clear that you have different arrangements with different people, he says. "In nearly all cases, people regard that as an example of your integrity as a journalist. It doesn't cause them to say, 'I'm not talking to you unless you tell me who else you're talking to.' If that happens, you have to ask yourself, what does this source want and why are they trying to manipulate me in this way?"

CONFRONTING TARGETS OF AN INVESTIGATION

Opinions vary about when to confront the subject of an investigation. Some reporters prefer to make the earliest possible contact in case they're on the wrong track. Others prefer to wait until they're nearly ready to publish, to avoid the chance that a tip-off undercuts the investigation by allowing the subject to get out a competing story, for example. At the very least, you need to give the subjects of your investigation a reasonable amount of time to respond to the evidence you've gathered, and to ensure that you ask them about every charge that will appear in the story.

Interview strategies differ as well. I've found it's best to start out with general questions and gradually become more focused until I get to the main allegations, lest the person decide not to talk at all. Avoiding charged language and loaded questions is likely to prove more successful at getting answers than something like, "Isn't it true you've been secretly taking money from the fossil fuel industry for years while denying climate change?" Instead, start with something like, "My reporting shows that you've consulted for the energy industry in the past. Can you describe that work?"

Subjects may simply deny any charges you present, or they may respond with threats. But when they start talking, don't interrupt. Ask open-ended questions (a good idea in general) to maximize the likelihood of getting useful information. If they pivot from your questions to avoid answering, keep asking until you get what you want, or can fairly report that they refused to answer. If you have trouble securing an interview, you might tell the source that the story is strong enough to run without them, but you'd like to give them a chance to tell their side of the story.

However egregious you find someone's behavior, remember it's not your job to pass judgment. You're there to get information. And that includes information that reveals moral complexity. Clearly defined heroes and villains make great movie fare, but we live in a world where good people sometimes do bad things and vice versa. Embrace the complexity in what your sources tell you and you'll end up painting a more nuanced and a more credible portrait of the people in your story.

MIT's Deborah Blum says one of the "big myths" about investigative reporters is that they bully and browbeat people to extract information. "I'm almost never nicer than when I'm an investigative reporter," she says. "I recognize that it's tricky terrain and I don't booby-trap people. If people ask, 'Am I going to like this story?' I usually say, 'I can't promise you that, but I promise it will be fair and I promise it will be accurate and I promise if I have any questions, I'll check back with you.'"

It's important to remember that you're dealing with people's lives, Blum says. "Part of the way you get past people saying 'I didn't like what you wrote' is that you treat people really well, you're honest and tell them, 'Here's the higher truth of it,'" she says. "And you have to be phenomenally accurate."

It can be intimidating and even a little scary to confront

someone you've discovered has done something wrong or illegal, especially for science journalists who may be accustomed to interviewing people who love to talk about themselves and their work. But remember why you started the investigation: to inform readers about a matter of public interest. Your first loyalty lies with your readers, not your sources. Prepare for the interview, ask your questions in a straightforward, open-ended manner and listen carefully to what they have to say. Tell them you may need to get back to them with follow-up questions. And don't forget to thank them for their time.

References

1. Liza Gross, "At California Psychiatric Hospitals, Epidemic of Patients' Assaults on Staff Goes Untreated," KQED, Oct. 3, 2016. https://www.kqed.org/stateofhealth/240260/at-california-psychiatric-hospitals-epidemic-of-patients-assaults-on-staff-goes-untreated
2. Valerie Brown and Elizabeth Grossman, "Why the United States Leaves Deadly Chemicals on the Market," In These Times, Nov. 2, 2015. http://inthesetimes.com/article/18504/epa_government_scientists_and_chemical_industry_links_influence_regulations
3. John Upton, "The Injustice of Atlantic City's Floods," Climate Central, May 10, 2017. http://www.climatecentral.org/news/the-injustice-of-atlantic-citys-floods-21434

End Notes

- ✓ Adopt a "documents state of mind," which assumes that a document may exist to prove or disprove your premise and assumptions.
- ✓ Cultivate a "data state of mind" by asking questions to quantify the problem you're investigating.
- ✓ Come up with a strategy and organize your reporting plans on a whiteboard or spreadsheet to help you track progress.
- ✓ Know what is exempt from state and federal public records laws so you don't waste time asking for records that aren't available to the public.
- ✓ Don't assume government officials know what records their agency keeps. Be prepared to spend time reviewing forms, databases and reports to figure out what you can ask for.
- ✓ Keep a reporting and data diary so you can easily redo analyses and retrieve information.
- ✓ Do background checks on key sources to avoid unwelcome surprises that could undercut their credibility after the story runs.
- ✓ Clearly state your reporting aims when approaching vulnerable sources and explain that you can't guarantee a story's outcomes.
- ✓ If someone insists on speaking off the record, consider that they may have their own agenda.
- ✓ Give subjects a reasonable amount of time to respond to any charges in the story.

[4]

FINDING INVESTIGATIVE STORIES: HOW THEY DID IT

SCIENCE WRITERS TEND TO BE a curious lot, drawn to the field to understand how the world works. When you redirect that curiosity to consider why things don't work as they should, you're more likely to find investigative stories. You can cultivate that curiosity the same way you would for any story: by brainstorming, saving anything remotely intriguing in a clip file, scanning news for open questions or chatting with friends, family and even random people on the street.

You can also try a more targeted approach to get story ideas by reading competing interest statements on papers in contentious fields, browsing databases that archive internal industry documents (e.g., toxicdocs.org), tracking industry payments to doctors (e.g., the Centers for Medicare and Medicaid Services Open Payments portal, https://www.cms.gov/openpayments/) or analyzing campaign contributions to politicians who promote anti-science views (e.g., followthemoney.org).

If the idea well runs dry, you might try a more systematic method for focusing your curiosity. Writing coach and Pulitzer Prize–winner Jacqui Banaszynski has come up with a strategy that encourages you to "live your life in the form of a question" [1]. This involves approaching everything you encounter in your professional and personal life with an eye toward digging deeper. Hear a story at a dinner party about someone's relative who fell for a shady medical treatment? Check it out. See a notice about a class-action lawsuit charging a chemical manufacturer with poisoning a community? Contact the law firm to find out more. Whenever you finish a story, jot down any questions you can think of, then check that list the next morning, and again days, even weeks later. If anything still piques your interest, Banaszynski says, you may have the makings of a good enterprise piece.

Make sure you also have a system for capturing your ideas. Compelling story ideas invariably pop into your head when you're taking a walk or drifting off to sleep, so it pays to keep a pad and pen handy at all times.

One of the first lessons writers learn is that a topic is not a story. (For an in-depth primer on finding story ideas, see Chapter 2 of "The Science Writers' Handbook" [2].) No matter how interesting the topic, if you don't explore it through characters who encounter some sort of problem that's eventually resolved (for good or bad), you don't have a story. Among the first things investigative reporters learn is that there's always a story behind the story, and that you should never take anything at face value. Investigative stories require intense curiosity and skepticism as well as a willingness to come up with your own hypothesis, gather as much evidence as you need to disprove or confirm your hypothesis and turn all that evidence into a compelling narrative.

Focus your investigation

Investigative stories also require a clear premise to guide your reporting so you don't waste a lot of time on a fishing expedition. If you had unlimited time, you might cast a wide net to search for evidence of wrongdoing by some individual or organization. But you're more likely to succeed if you know what you're looking for.

If you have an idea for an investigation, the first thing you should do is figure out what's been written on the topic, as you would for any story. That starts with simple online searches and then asking sources if anyone else has talked to them about the same issue.

If you're confident you're in unmapped territory, start by formulating a specific question. As Joe Bergantino tells his students, you have to formulate a specific question that allows you to conduct a targeted investigation, which means you need to do enough preliminary research to figure out if there's a story there.

That key question will provide an overarching framework that guides your reporting by leading to supporting questions and sources and materials that can answer them. A few examples:

- Have state officials failed to meet their obligation to protect vulnerable communities from toxic exposures? (Start by looking at health advisories or standards for the exposure of interest, then check EPA databases to see which communities exceed those limits.)
- Have state psychiatric hospitals really improved safety for staff and patients as officials have claimed? (Start by obtaining aggressive incident data from the state and compare that to workers' compensation claims and any other data or reports you can identify that might track injuries or absences.)
- Does a group claiming to help journalists and the public make sense of contested evidence truly promote science in the public interest? (Start by reviewing their materials to see if you detect a pattern of bias over time.)

After you've done enough preliminary reporting to formulate a question, try asking yourself this series of questions suggested by Banaszynski:

- What's my story about?
- What's my key point?

- Why does it matter here and now?
- What does it say about life, the world, the times we live in?

If you work through these questions and still think you have an investigation worth pursuing, see if you can describe your story in six words or less. For example: EPA fails to enforce civil rights. "Sound science" group fronts for industry. If you can't do it, you may need to do more research.

One way to come up with investigative science story ideas is to flip your focus from the people doing science to the people affected by science. Can you identify winners and losers? Can you find cases where corporate practices or systemic policy failures affect the well-being of a community? Rather than asking how something works, ask how well it's working. Instead of looking at who's getting grants, ask if there are disparities in grant funding and if areas critical to the public interest are underfunded.

When you start thinking about how science is supposed to be practiced and used, you're likely to see any number of instances where things go wrong: fraud, scientific misconduct, conflicts of interest, sexual harassment, industry distortion of science to protect profits, communities at risk from emerging contaminants, policies that fail to use the best available science, unsafe medical interventions and charlatans peddling pseudoscience.

DEVELOP A MINIMUM AND MAXIMUM STORY

Once you've formulated a question, you can lay out a reporting plan to test your ideas. (See Chapter 5 for more on testing and verifying hypotheses.)

It's tempting to imagine that your ambitious reporting plan will pay off, but prudence dictates that you have an alternate strategy. As you're doing your preliminary reporting, think about the maximum story you're shooting for as well as a minimum story you can fall back on if you can't get all the materials you need.

Say you're assessing risks from chemical exposures throughout your state. The maximum story might show that several low-income minority communities suffer much higher rates of disease than more affluent neighborhoods because they live near chemical facilities with lax regulatory oversight. A minimum story might show that a single facility has a history of failing to enforce safety rules. Evaluate your material as you go and write nut graphs to see if you already have a story.

TAKE THE LONG VIEW

When young reporters ask Charles Piller of Science how he broke into investigative work, he warns them there are no shortcuts. Staff writers already have enormous demands on their time and freelancers need assignments that pay the bills. You may need to work nights and weekends to develop a story to the point where it seems feasible and there's a clear path to getting critical information. "If you have passion for digging deeper and for trying to do investigations," he says, "you have to chip away at them [knowing] it might take you months to get to the point where you have enough knowledge to pitch it to an editor."

Any good reporting has to employ a degree of skepticism about the relevance and reality of a given topic to avoid writing clickbait "chocolate cures cancer" stories. "Investigative reporting will generally take that further and also originate ideas to examine issues that aren't necessarily part of the flow of news," Piller says. "You want to look deeper into the motivations and interests of the parties that are exploring a particular scientific idea or promoting a product or a new scientific development, and also examine the range of motives that might be behind them and whether they're trustworthy or have holes in them."

That's the approach Piller took in a series for STAT that investigated a company marketing an unproven opioid-addiction risk test [3]. The company, called Proove Biosciences, claimed its test could predict with very high accuracy whether a person would abuse opioid pain pills based on a genetic profile and a questionnaire. Piller saw many stories that extolled the virtues of the test, which could have helped doctors determine whether they might ultimately harm a patient by prescribing opioids. But when he spoke to experts in the field and examined the techniques the company used, he discovered the claims it was making were unsupported by the state of scientific knowledge.

"So the question then became, what is the bigger issue here?" Piller says. The first thing he did was write a story ("Called 'Hogwash,' a Gene Test for Addiction Risk Exploits Opioid Fears" [4]) that examined the scientific validity of the claims and put a spotlight on the company and the product it was selling. "Then, what so often is the case if you dig deeper under the surface," he says, "you discover the broader motives, the more important elements of the story."

After the story appeared, people came out of the woodwork to tell Piller there was much more going on. Over a period of months, he spoke with employees, former employees and others who knew the internal workings of the company. Those interviews allowed him to write an exposé detailing a wide range of unscrupulous business practices.

"I was able to write a story that exposed questionable and apparently fraudulent billing, massive errors in the testing process, exploitation of patients, unnecessary testing, exploitation of the clinical trial registration process to boost revenues," he says. "It was only possible to do that by taking a long view and realizing that for many, many scientific stories there are layers of knowledge to be gained, and you have to dig beneath the surface in order to understand the business, political, social and legal context of the claims that are being made."

The last story in Piller's series reported that Proove Biosciences' CEO left the company after it had been placed under court-ordered receivership as part of a criminal investigation.

POKE AROUND IN DATABASES

Intercept reporter Sharon Lerner knew she wanted to write about air pollution, so she scrolled through the Environmental Protection Agency's National Air Toxics Assessment (NATA) [5] data and noticed something peculiar. Estimates of health risks from air toxics are reported at the census tract level in each state. Lerner saw that the cancer risk from air pollution was close to zero per million in most parts of the country, with most census tracts ranging between 0 and 1. But one tract had a "crazy high" number — 777 — and Lerner wanted to know why.

"When I looked more closely at the data, I saw that was due almost entirely to emissions of a chemical called chloroprene," she says. "That took me to the factory that made it — and the community living right next to it."

Chloroprene is a building block of the synthetic rubber neoprene, which gives stability and flexibility to a wide array of products, from mouse pads to wetsuits. In 1969, DuPont started making neoprene, and releasing chloroprene, in St. John the Baptist Parish, Louisiana — where Lerner saw the extremely high cancer risk. To learn about the chemical's health effects, she checked the EPA's Integrated Risk Information System (IRIS) [6], which had evaluated the chemical in 2010 and deemed it a likely human carcinogen. In addition, the IRIS evaluation included references to a wealth of studies going back decades.

Lerner also took advantage of internal DuPont documents, released through discovery from other cases. Those documents revealed that DuPont had known about chloroprene's dangers decades before — and hid that knowledge to protect its interests.

Draft budget proposals from the Trump administration that had been leaked to the press showed that IRIS was on the "top of the list" of environmental programs to cut. That provided a compelling frame for what Lerner found by scrolling through the NATA data. Her story, "The Plant Next Door," explored how towns already plagued by pollution would suffer even more if the budget cuts for air pollution monitoring passed [7]. (Congress ultimately rejected Trump's plan to slash the EPA's budget.)

Lerner worked with an academic science adviser throughout the reporting to help her locate and interpret documents and technical details. The adviser helped her understand how the EPA comes up with air pollution risk estimates and what they mean. But ultimately, the story was about the people who were living in the fallout of chemical pollution. To get a better sense of the risks facing the people living near the factory, Lerner printed out a map showing the census tracts and jotted down the NATA estimates for each tract as a reference for when she visited the region and interviewed residents.

Lerner advises anyone interested in doing a similar type of story to talk to as many people as possible. "It was so important for me to speak with as many residents as I could and listen to their stories. Even if some people don't make it into the piece, it's critical to hear about what it is like to live in a place that you are just briefly visiting," she says. "I almost always feel like I have way too much material, which I've come to realize must actually be the right amount."

Team up to expand your expertise

In addition to involving considerable effort, investigative stories require enough expertise to understand how things are supposed to work so you can tell when they go wrong. If you're on a beat, you've likely developed a level of expertise in a field that will help you notice when something's not quite right and see patterns others might miss. Even so, it can be extremely time-consuming to try to master the intricacies of both the policy and science in an investigative story.

Independent journalist Valerie Brown has a long history of writing about chemicals, environmental health and regulation. So did her colleague, Lizzie Grossman, a longtime environmental health reporter who died of cancer in 2017. But Grossman gravitated toward the esoteric aspects of policymaking while Brown preferred getting into the weeds of the science. They had a habit of exchanging ideas and comparing notes about story ideas, and discovered they both had an interest in an arcane method to assess health effects of chemical exposures favored by regulatory toxicologists called physiologically based pharmacokinetic (PBPK) modeling.

"Lizzie was into the weirdness of PBPK filtering into chemicals screening," says Brown, "and between us, we came up with a pitch for ITT's Leonard C. Goodman grant program." (The program, run by In These Times, provides editorial and financial support for in-depth investigative projects that challenge the status quo.)

Brown and Grossman knew there was a rift between academic researchers who studied the effects of chemical exposures and regulatory toxicologists who assessed exposure risks through PBPK computer simulations. The academics, mostly endocrinologists, developmental biologists and epidemiologists, were accumulating evidence through direct observations that many chemicals caused an array of harmful effects in living things. The PBPK modelers, by contrast, tended to downplay or cast doubt on chemicals' health effects, ultimately helping to delay regulation. The two camps had become so polarized they routinely traded insults in public forums.

Brown and Grossman decided to figure out how regulators

came to rely on PBPK modeling. They hypothesized that the PBPK modelers had chemical industry connections, since their findings invariably favored the industry's interests. So they started backgrounding the PBPK modelers and looking for connections. "We looked at every relevant industry website, searched PubMed for every study on PBPK, read reviews and critiques by academic researchers and interviewed both regulatory toxicologists and independent or academic scientists," Brown says.

An effective way to build networks of industry connections is to find studies by the people you're interested in, and then check their co-authors, Brown adds. "In this case we found an extensive web of co-authors on industry-friendly studies. Typically, a first and corresponding author would list an academic affiliation, and other authors might work for a chemical company or a consultancy. Then we collected as many bios, CVs and other documents as we could find about these people, which revealed even more of the web. You can find out who was working with whom at what stage of their career, which allowed us to trace the PBPK system through successive generations of researchers."

That backgrounding technique allowed the pair to document an intricate network of industry-friendly scientists among regulatory agencies, corporations and consultancies. "Once we got on to the connections among the PBPK modelers, we began to see PBPK in a wider context," Brown says.

And that allowed them to trace the development of the chemical industry trade groups, the chemical consultancies and the PBPK modeling idea. Corporate interests began to control both the regulatory process and the science, they showed, by steering the field of regulatory toxicology toward downplaying the risk of toxic chemicals.

Their resulting story, "Why the United States Leaves Deadly Chemicals on the Market," revealed a revolving door between government and the chemical industry that led the EPA to rely on "easily manipulated research" that sanctioned the use of toxic substances in a slew of everyday products [8].

Brown recognizes that journalists who are expected to do quick-turnaround stories or write to strict word lengths probably can't tackle this type of investigative story. But even so, she says, you can push your editor to let you write about the same subject from different angles so you can present a deeper picture of what's going on.

"I think for real investigative journalism, you have to be interested in long-form explanatory writing," Brown says. "It helps if you lose track of time when you're digging through information, trying to find the right sources, writing down questions your piece needs to answer. That means you've found your right livelihood."

Capitalize on Tips

Once people know that you do investigative reporting, and see that you produce solid work, they're likely to come to you with tips. Reporters sometimes receive anonymous tips from people who've discovered something they think the public should know. In rare cases, a reporter might receive a treasure trove of secret company documents detailing malfeasance, as Lowell Bergman did in the early 1990s, when someone dropped a cache of thousands of internal Philip Morris papers on his doorstep showing that the tobacco giant had developed a self-extinguishing cigarette that could save lives but decided to shelve the product. (Bergman would later be played by Al Pacino in a film about the episode, "The Insider.") Less dramatic tips may come from regular sources or strangers, including activists, private citizens, policy experts, scientists, whistleblowers and lawyers.

A tip is just the beginning of the reporting process, no matter how trusted the source. Treat tips as ideas to investigate and (if possible) verify, using documents and other materials that can help you decide whether to dismiss an idea or pursue it further.

Barry Yeoman, a freelance journalist based in Durham, North Carolina, received a tip from a plaintiff in a lawsuit that ultimately led to his piece for Audubon, "The Inside Story of Shell's Arctic Assault" [9]. Several organizations had sued the administration of President George W. Bush for offering some 29 million acres of public lands in the Arctic for oil and gas leasing so oil giant Royal Dutch Shell could drill in the Chukchi Sea. The source, who worked for one of the plaintiff organizations, suggested that a number of public documents showed the Interior Department had bowed to pressure from Shell to accelerate review for the leases and accede to the energy giant's timeline.

Earthjustice, a nonprofit environmental law organization that was representing the plaintiffs, had secured hundreds of government documents through legal action and the federal Freedom of Information Act (FOIA). Yeoman's source told him Earthjustice was willing to share both the FOIA'd documents and the administrative record, a paper trail of all the information a federal agency uses to make a policy decision. (Federal agencies are required to provide electronic access, through FOIA "reading rooms," to basic agency records as well as any records disclosed in response to a FOIA request that the agency "determines have become or are likely to become the subject of subsequent requests for substantially the same records." The ease of navigating and retrieving documents, however, varies widely across agencies.)

"The source also suggested that there were interesting documents from the U.S. Fish and Wildlife Service (USFWS) chronicling Shell's fight against the mandatory 15-mile buffer between active rigs," Yeoman says.

With more than 700 documents from Earthjustice, Yeoman

had to figure out what the story was. "My starting question was this: did Shell successfully pressure the United States government to accelerate the process that would ultimately allow the company to drill in the Chukchi Sea? Before I reviewed the documents, I honestly did not know the answer to the question. If the answer was 'no,' I was prepared to jettison the narrative and write a less investigative article about the fight over drilling in the Chukchi."

Yeoman gathered a massive cache of documents in the course of testing his question. An Earthjustice staffer highlighted a subset of the 700 documents the group considered important, but Yeoman also waded through unhighlighted documents to make sure he didn't miss anything relevant. He then obtained public documents from the websites of a wide range of government agencies that might have played a role in the issue — including the Bureau of Ocean Energy Management (the Interior Department agency in charge of approving Shell's oil leases and exploration plan), USFWS, the Bureau of Safety and Environmental Enforcement, the EPA, the Government Accountability Office, the Department of Interior's Office of Inspector General and the U.S. Coast Guard.

He also drew on court documents, academic journal articles, research by industry, environmental organizations, academics and neutral policy groups as well as news articles. All together, the materials Yeoman gathered helped support his original hypothesis that the regulatory system was geared toward meeting the needs of the oil industry while ignoring the potential impacts on climate change and sensitive ecosystems.

And here's a nice illustration of investigative journalism's charge to challenge conventional wisdom: Although environmental groups first sued the Bush administration to stop the Shell oil lease sales, it was President Obama's White House that greased the wheels to help the oil giant. As Yeoman reported: "These efforts to accommodate a multinational energy company happened under the watch of President Barack Obama, who is reviled, ironically, by drilling advocates and eager to cement his legacy as a climate warrior."

Partner with Scientists

A critical element of investigative science journalism involves keeping a healthy distance from your sources and viewing the scientific enterprise with skepticism. But that doesn't mean you can't work with scientists as advisers or partners on a project to help you uncover dodgy practices or policies, analyze data or interpret complex technical information. Scientists can also help you use science to uncover widespread problems or disparate impacts on vulnerable communities.

Reporter John Upton is in the unique position of working at an organization that employs both journalists and scientists. At Climate Central, a nonprofit that studies and reports on climate change and its impact on the public, Upton can coordinate with scientific researchers to tell a story based on their work.

He got the idea for "The Injustice of Atlantic City's Floods" by perusing spreadsheets that Climate Central scientists had produced for a research project analyzing flood risks in coastal cities [10]. "Some cities popped out as facing higher risks, including Atlantic City," says Upton. The town is not only close to Climate Central's offices, making site visits convenient, but it's also in the throes of an economic crisis.

While the scientists wrote up their findings and sent them to a journal for peer review, Upton reported on flooding in Atlantic City, with a goal of determining whether the economic crisis was affecting adaptation efforts. "My story revealed vast inequality in flooding protections provided by governments for rich and poor, which inspired a new research agenda by our scientists that's starting to look at sea-level rise as a local economic issue. So we've got a nice loop going now involving journalism and science."

Upton consulted the scientists to make sure he was interpreting the data correctly and to discuss what his reporting revealed, but otherwise reported the story independently. In this case, he also used one of the scientists as a source. "Our chief scientist, Ben Strauss, a co-author of the paper, is a thought leader on sea-level rise, and I sat down with him for a formal interview halfway through the project. I ended up including some of his quotes in the story. They were strong and insightful, so it was an easy decision to include them."

Upton is well aware that most journalists don't have scientist colleagues, but says the approach can be replicated for any science that involves impacts on humans, from mental health to conservation. He suggests developing strong relationships with leading scientists and asking them to keep you advised of upcoming papers. "Better yet, join them for fieldwork. When they submit a paper for peer review, ask for an embargoed copy of the manuscript and take it from there. The peer review process can take months, allowing plenty of time for field reporting and writing."

That lengthy lead time can also make it tough to schedule publication well in advance, he acknowledges. Some editors may be more willing than others to wait for a paper to come out.

For Upton, investigative science stories typically involve puncturing a scientific myth. Special interest groups can easily create science-related myths, he says, which scientists can unwittingly sustain if they fail to question an underlying assumption. "The most successful and regrettable myths are perpetuated by the media, often tacitly pushed along by special interest groups, and stated as fact. A few years ago I produced a series for Climate Central showing why it's dangerously wrong to assume that burning wood in power plants releases no carbon dioxide overall, which is a myth that some in the energy industry push aggressively, aided by some forestry scientists.

"Find those myths," Upton says. "Puncture them by explaining the truth, and showing why it matters, with clear and forceful writing and compelling anecdotes and quotes."

You may find that scientists are eager to collaborate on an investigative project, as I did for an environmental justice story on pesticide use near California schools. No one would be surprised that pesticide exposures are higher in farmworking communities, which are predominantly Latino, than in other places. I wanted to find a way to show this disparity in a new light, so people might take notice. Knowing scientists who worked on this issue helped me accomplish what I set out to do. They helped me design my investigation and interpret my results.

California keeps records of all the pesticides sprayed in all 58 counties, but that's a massive amount of data. I wanted to filter the data by the most harmful pesticides, based on toxicity and tendency to drift, to get a sense of who faced the highest risk. So I contacted health experts who worked on pesticide issues in these communities and asked if they had any ideas about how to do this. I discovered that the state of California was in the midst of studying agricultural pesticide use near schools and had actually identified 60-some pesticides that met my criteria. That helped in two ways: it not only cut down the number of records I'd have to analyze, but also allowed me to hold the state accountable for allowing kids to be exposed to chemicals public officials knew caused harm.

Yet even with my smaller datasets, I ran into a problem: pesticide data are mapped to an arcane geography that doesn't correspond to where people live. I needed geographic information system experts who could convert the pesticide data to ZIP codes so I could see which communities faced the highest risk. I knew

Jonathan London, an environmental justice and policy expert at the Center for Regional Change at the University of California, Davis, had a team who could do this. He agreed to help.

Epidemiologists I knew had helped me figure out how to frame my investigation, and London helped me analyze the data. As a result, I discovered that there has been a dramatic rise in pesticide use in California communities that are predominantly Latino. And not only that: I found that families in one of the communities with the highest levels of toxic pesticides had filed a Title VI Civil Rights Act complaint with the EPA several years earlier, alleging that state regulators had violated federal civil rights laws by approving permits allowing pesticide use near their children's schools, where kids were mostly Latino.

This original Title VI complaint and the EPA's own analysis showed that the kids were disproportionately impacted, but the complaint had languished for years, finally resolving without relief for the families. My investigation, which ran in The Nation as "Fields of Toxic Pesticides Surround the Schools of Ventura County — Are They Poisoning the Students?" [11] showed that growers' use of toxic chemicals had skyrocketed after the regulatory agencies said the issue had been resolved.

Though I didn't work on the investigation full-time, I did spend several months working with data, learning how to use software programs to acquire and analyze data and coordinating with scientists to confirm my interpretations of the data and the evidence I'd gathered.

All that time and effort paid off. I presented the findings of my Nation story to California state senators and representatives at a meeting at the Capitol about pesticide use near schools. In January 2018, the state adopted stricter rules on pesticide use near schools, though public health scientists and activists say they're not yet strict enough.

But perhaps most gratifying was a note I received from the young woman I featured in the story, Dayane Zuñiga. "It was such a pleasure being part of this story!! Thank you for the opportunity!!" Zuñiga told me in a Facebook post. "Trust that many great things happened once this story got published!!"

She also asked me to continue to tell these kinds of stories, to unearth injustices and give a platform to those who don't have a voice. And that might be the best explanation for why investigative journalism is so important.

References

1. Jacqui Banaszynski, "Journalistic Jeopardy: Live Your Life in the Form of a Question," (Story Idea Generation — 10 Tips.) http://www.jacquibanaszynski.com/resources-for-writers/
2. Thomas Hayden and Michelle Nijhuis, editors, "The Science Writers' Handbook: Everything You Need to Know to Pitch, Publish, and Prosper in the Digital Age," Da Capo Press, 2013.
3. STAT Proove Biosciences series. https://www.statnewcom/?s=proove+biosciences
4. Charles Piller, "Called 'Hogwash,' a Gene Test for Addiction Risk Exploits Opioid Fears," STAT, Dec. 13, 2016. https://www.statnews.com/2016/12/13/proove-opioid-risk-test/
5. National Air Toxics Assessment, Environmental Protection Agency. https://www.epa.gov/national-air-toxics-assessment
6. Integrated Risk Information System, Environmental

Protection Agency.
https://www.epa.gov/iris

7. Sharon Lerner, "The Plant Next Door," The Intercept, March 24, 2017.
https://theintercept.com/2017/03/24/a-louisiana-town-plagued-by-pollution-shows-why-cuts-to-the-epa-will-be-measured-in-illnesses-and-deaths/
8. Valerie Brown and Elizabeth Grossman, "Why the United States Leaves Deadly Chemicals on the Market," In These Times, Nov. 2, 2015.
http://inthesetimes.com/article/18504/epa_government_scientists_and_chemical_industry_links_influence_regulations
9. Barry Yeoman, "The Inside Story of Shell's Arctic Assault," Audubon, Jan.-Feb. 2016.
http://www.audubon.org/magazine/january-february-2016/the-inside-story-shells-arctic-assault
10. John Upton, "The Injustice of Atlantic City's Floods," Climate Central, May 10, 2017.
http://www.climatecentral.org/news/the-injustice-of-atlantic-citys-floods-21434
11. Liza Gross, "Fields of Toxic Pesticides Surround the Schools of Ventura County — Are They Poisoning the Students?" The Nation, April 6, 2015.
https://www.thenation.com/article/fields-toxic-pesticides-surround-schools-ventura-county-are-they-poisoning-students/

END NOTES

- ✓ Create a system to capture your ideas.
- ✓ Look for the story behind the story.
- ✓ Start with a clear premise and do enough reporting to ensure there's a story worth your time and effort.
- ✓ Once you're confident your story is worth pursuing, formulate a question to guide your investigation.
- ✓ If you can't describe your story in six words or less, you may need to do more research.
- ✓ Hedge your bets by planning for a minimum story in case your maximum story doesn't pan out.
- ✓ Talk to as many people as possible to fully understand how the problems you've unearthed affect them.
- ✓ Treat tips as ideas to investigate to decide whether to pursue further.
- ✓ Watch for stories that might puncture scientific myths or challenge conventional wisdom.

[5]

THE SCIENCE OF GETTING IT RIGHT

Objectivity is not the absence of a point of view [but] a disciplined unity of method transparently conveyed.
— "The Elements of Journalism"

THE WORRIES THAT DOG ALL REPORTERS shift into overdrive on an investigative story. You might worry that you treated a target unfairly. Or that you missed a line of inquiry that could have led to a smoking gun. Or even worse, that you made factual errors. That's what keeps Science's Charles Piller up at night. "I spend countless hours fact-checking, bulletproofing my stories, making sure that before anything becomes public, I've checked every word in that story repeatedly to make sure it's correct and precise," he says.

It's impossible to avoid reporting errors entirely, given the sheer volume of stories produced and the pressure to meet deadlines. In most cases, you run a correction and move on. But when subjects of your investigation can weaponize even the smallest error, no matter how tangential, to discredit your entire story, accuracy assumes paramount importance. "The accuracy of the smallest thing is a proxy for the accuracy of your entire argument and the entire body of work that you're presenting," Piller says. "Being incredibly careful and scrupulous in everything you do associated with validating your claims is not just important, but you're lost if you don't do that."

There's no one way to ensure your story is airtight. But there are techniques that can help you gather and analyze relevant facts while testing their accuracy in isolation and in the context of your working assumptions about a story. They help you approach verification like a science, formulating and testing hypotheses much the way a scientist does.

In "The New Precision Journalism" [1], computer-assisted reporting pioneer Philip Meyer writes that both journalism and science attempt to produce shared knowledge and understanding: "Reporters, like scientists, are in the business of reality testing, examining the existing theories, thinking through their consequences, developing related hypotheses that can be operationalized (that is, tested), and putting them to the test."

The idea, Meyer argues, is to focus on the objective validity of facts rather than on the objectivity of the person reporting them. The best way to arrive at "objectifiable facts," as opposed to objective journalists, he says, is "to push journalism toward science, incorporating both the powerful data-gathering and analysis tools of science and its disciplined search for verifiable truth."

In "The Elements of Journalism" [2], Bill Kovach and Tom Rosenstiel compare the importance and spirit of transparency in journalism to the process of replication in science: "Explain how you learned something and why you believe it — so the audience can do the same. In science, the reliability of an experiment, or its objectivity, is defined by whether someone else can replicate the experiment. In journalism, only by explaining how we know what we know can we approximate this idea of people being able, if they are of a mind to, to replicate the reporting."

MANAGE YOUR BIASES

The fear of getting it wrong can focus the mind on nailing down the facts, as well as the context surrounding those facts. But you also have to account for biases that can arise when you spend weeks or months investigating people or organizations you suspect of subverting the public interest. Your personal biases, and sense of outrage at perceived injustices, may guide your choice of subject. But they can also cloud the way you gather and interpret evidence.

At the start of an investigation, confront your biases head on by writing down any preconceptions you have about the subjects you're investigating. Do you have strong feelings about anyone you're investigating? Is that influencing the way you interpret information? Check the list as your reporting proceeds to see if any biases you've listed have changed. Think about whether you've tried to find information that might neutralize those biases or if your reporting has only served to confirm them. (See Chapter 6 for more on confirmation bias.)

One way to get a handle on your biases is to report against them, Washington Post media columnist (and former New York Times public editor) Margaret Sullivan told the Columbia Journalism Review [3]. "That is, include the reporting that has a chance of proving you wrong, not just confirming what you already think or think that you know," she said. "At the very least, this will allow you to know in advance what the objections to a story might be. It tends to make reporting more fair — and more bulletproof."

BE PREPARED TO SHIFT GEARS

As noted in Chapter 4, you need to do background research to make sure you've got a story worth investing in, and formulate an overarching question to guide your reporting. Then, once you start reporting, it's critical to keep an open mind in the face of evidence that contradicts your working assumptions, so you can shift gears and change your assumptions — and your story — if necessary. The goal is to report in a way that can prove or disprove your hypothesis and the assumptions underlying it, as scientists do. Just as writing coaches tell you to "kill your darlings," be prepared to reject your assumptions, even those based on preliminary reporting.

It can be scary and frustrating to realize after weeks of reporting that your central premise is wrong. That happened to me when I was reporting on disparate pesticide exposures in California. I'd pitched the story, based on preliminary reporting, thinking that the communities exposed to the most dangerous pesticides would be predominantly Latino towns in Fresno County in the Central Valley. My assumption was based on talking to sources and on data showing that Fresno County had the highest total pesticide use in the state going back years. But as my data analysis progressed, I realized the highest levels of dangerous pesticides were being used around a Southern California town called Oxnard.

This caused me some consternation, at first, because I'd already done field reporting in Fresno and had expected to anchor my story in the experiences of the people and communities there. But as I looked into the places flagged by the data, I found an even better story: Latino families in Oxnard were well aware that their kids went to schools with much higher levels of toxic pesticides than white kids and had filed a complaint against the EPA to seek relief from these disparate exposures. The complaint had been settled, but without reductions in pesticide use. And my data showed that the use of dangerous pesticides had risen dramatically after the settlement [4].

At first I didn't believe what the data were telling me. That's how conceptual errors can creep in: you settle on a larger narrative, either one you've created or one in keeping with conventional wisdom or presumed "facts" everyone takes for granted, and you expect the information you gather to fit that narrative. It's critical to report against that narrative, as Sullivan suggests, to look at the facts through a lens that questions your expectations.

If evidence you've gathered contradicts your assumptions, try to come up with alternative explanations for what you've found. Look for the simplest explanation. If you have to imagine a series of conditions to make it fit, it probably doesn't. If you can't figure out how to explain what you found, ask experts for help. It took me a day of analyzing and reanalyzing my pesticide data to conclude that my original hypothesis was wrong and that the data pointed to higher risks in a different part of the state. There just wasn't another plausible explanation.

For Science's Piller, skepticism serves as a guiding light in the reporting process. "The origin of these stories is often skepticism, of what you're hearing, what people are saying, what they're doing," he says. "By the same token, it's our obligation as investigative reporters to be equally skeptical of our own assumptions as the reporting evolves, to challenge ourselves to look at what we've found and think it through in a skeptical way so that we can test those assumptions."

RULES TO REPORT BY

Kovach and Rosenstiel offer a conceptual framework for taking a scientific approach that ensures you're not just gathering facts that fit your hypothesis. They distill the science of reporting, the process of verification, into five broad principles:

- Don't add anything that wasn't there (that is, don't make stuff up).
- Never deceive your audience.
- Reveal your methods and motives.
- Do your own reporting.
- Be humble.

These are basic rules that apply to all journalism, but it's worth considering them in the context of investigative reporting. When you're dealing with a lot of data and statistics, there's a natural tendency to want to make sure you have enough drama to hold a reader's interest. It seems obvious but still bears noting: never add details for drama or color that you can't prove. Unless a source told you what she was thinking, don't pretend you know. It's not a literary flourish, it's making stuff up. And it's handing subjects of your investigation ammunition to use against you.

Efforts to expose corruption or abuse come with great responsibility. Exercise humility. If someone tells you something that undercuts your main premise or your editor questions your assumptions, take them seriously. You can always start another line of inquiry. It's much harder to repair your reputation — or live with the consequences of ruining someone's life based on faulty assumptions.

You can also deceive by insinuating that you know more than you do or by giving a source more authority and credibility than they deserve. Tell readers what you don't know as well as the limits of your sources' knowledge, to avoid misrepresenting or overstating the facts.

Be Original and Transparent

Ensuring that you don't overstate what you know depends on two critical, overlapping elements of investigative journalism: base your investigation on your own original reporting, and tell your readers as much as possible about how you know what you're reporting. Doing your own original reporting means that you're not relying on someone else's judgment calls — judgments you might not agree with or be able to defend. It also allows you to give readers the information they need to decide for themselves whether to trust the information, how it was obtained and whether you are a reliable narrator.

Barry Yeoman and his Audubon editors decided to tell readers high up in his story about how the Interior Department bowed to Shell's push for Arctic oil leases where they obtained the primary documents [5]: "... an Audubon investigation based on government documents — some filed in court and others obtained by Earthjustice, a nonprofit environmental law organization, through the Freedom of Information Act..." They also hyperlinked the documents so readers could evaluate the evidence for themselves. Yeoman says he prefers not to "clunk up the narrative with too much inside baseball," but wants to give readers enough information about the reporting process to see that he's calling balls and strikes fairly. (For more on transparency, see Chapter 6).

I provide relevant information on sources that might bear on their point of view and avoid vague attributions like "experts say," a formulation that's particularly unhelpful when dealing with controversy. How many experts? Which ones? Do they have a bias or a stake in a particular point of view? Are they credible? Is their expertise in a relevant field? If you're reporting on a polarized issue like an emerging public health threat, for example, and one set of "experts" repeatedly dismisses all available evidence of harm while another group expresses concern, look into the experts' backgrounds and affiliations to see if there's anything that might bias their perspective. These days, with stories distributed far and wide on social media platforms, if you don't reveal your sources' potential biases, chances are someone else will, which could reflect badly on you and your story.

KEEP DATA AND REPORTING DIARIES

Investigations typically involve gathering more information than you might for a typical explanatory story. It's critically important to take a systematic approach to both gathering and organizing your materials. I create a reporting diary, usually in a spreadsheet, that logs salient details about information I've gathered, including people I've talked to, records requests filed, scientific studies reviewed, court documents or data obtained and next steps. Some people even include detailed annotations of information contained in interviews or records.

If you're incorporating data in your investigation, make sure you get metadata describing the fields and write down where you got the data and any steps related to processing and analysis. You may think you'll remember how you derived a figure from a certain dataset, but that's unlikely when you have to reconstruct the analysis weeks or months later. Reporting and data diaries also make fact-checking much easier.

Every reporter has a different approach to organizing material. I tend to nest bookmarks in my browser (that is, start with general folders then create increasingly specific subfolders) that echo folders on my computer, which helps me locate information quickly. I also have hard copies of critical pieces of the story in files named after key concepts or people in the investigation. Yeoman used a similar nested folder system to organize the hundreds of documents he used for his Audubon story, with electronic folders exactly mirroring the hard copies of court documents he'd obtained. (For more tips on organizing data and documents, see Chapter 3.)

John Upton of Climate Central says he's "neurotically organized" when it comes to big projects. "I keep a Google doc with emails and interview notes from all of my sources, divided using headers and subheaders," he says.

"For the Atlantic City story I had nearly 70 pages of interview notes, divided into categories like 'residents,' 'scientists,' 'local government' and such. I downloaded the Google doc as a Word doc and stored it in a secure Dropbox folder as a backup. And I kept journal papers and voice files organized using folders and subfolders on my laptop, using file names that were easy to organize and identify, all of which I backed up regularly." (For more information on how to handle data, see "Getting a Handle on Data," below.)

VET SOURCES AND DOCUMENTS

Every story comes with its own set of challenges that require different strategies to get at the truth. But they should all start with a skepticism guided by the basic rule of reporting: assume nothing.

No matter where you get your information, says Piller, you have to ask yourself, "Are these comments I'm getting from people believable, and are these documents authentic?" And you have to be able to test these things. When sources started "coming out of the woodwork" after publication of Piller's first story on Proove Biosciences' shady genetics test [6], he came up with a process to vet what people told him. He interviewed dozens of former and then-current employees (the company went out of business after the series ran) but no one knew who else he was speaking to, so they couldn't consult with each other and compare notes.

"What I found was that when I was able to talk with lots and lots of people and hear very similar, overlapping consistent accounts of what was being done and the wrongdoing that was being described, it lent a lot of credibility to the idea that these things were going on," Piller says. "They didn't know who else was talking to me and they didn't know what other people were telling me, and yet the stories were extremely consistent."

Documents or data obtained from government agencies, whether through public records requests or their websites, are considered primary sources, at least for the purposes of attribution. If you give a fair and accurate account of an official government document, even though the information is wrong, the "Fair Report Privilege" (also known anachronistically as the newsman's privilege) generally exempts you from libel claims. That privilege doesn't apply to every government document, though, and it's good practice not to assume the information is correct just because it comes from the government.

It's critical to vet any government documents that are leaked, preferably by finding a source inside the relevant agency who can attest to their authenticity. The same holds for any other types of leaked documents. You can try asking people mentioned in the docs to validate them, says Piller, but they're not likely to cooperate if doing so makes them look bad.

Piller recommends a critical-mass approach to verifying documents. "One document is easy to falsify. A few documents might be easy to falsify. But hundreds or thousands of pages of documents about the same topic that can be cross-validated and viewed in context and compared with other records that are in the public domain are really, really difficult to falsify," he says.

GET A HANDLE ON DATA

Many investigative stories center around analyses of databases that identify trends or patterns that reveal matters of public interest. Sometimes reporters build their own databases by gathering information from diverse types of paper documents and entering it into spreadsheets (for example, Excel or Google Sheets) or database software (like Access or MySQL). Other times reporters acquire data from public records requests or by downloading datasets from government websites and soon discover that freely available public data can be a hot mess.

The first thing you should do with any dataset is inspect it to make sure it's "clean" — that is, names, places, dates and other entries are formatted and spelled the same way every time they appear. Such consistency rarely happens, though. More likely, you'll find the same information entered in every possible configuration, which wreaks havoc with your attempts to sort and filter to make sense of the data. Imagine you have a dataset showing corporate donations to companies and don't realize a company's name appears variously as Sound Science Incorporated, Sound Science, Inc. and SSC. You'll end up with random results that have little to do with what's actually in the dataset.

Making sure your data are clean usually involves a fair amount of processing. Luckily there are tools that can help you and don't require much skill to produce good results. A good choice is OpenRefine (formerly called Google Refine), a free, open source web-based tool that helps you standardize and reformat datasets with an intuitive, easy-to-use interface. It allows you to import data in various formats (for example, .csv, .xls, XML) from your computer, the cloud or urls. Once you create a project, you can access data-processing tools that allow you to go through each field to see variations on the same entry and take advantage of features that allow you to modify several hundred or thousands of cells at a time. All the revisions are saved, so if you make a mistake you can click "undo" as many times as you need to.

Data visualization tools can help you render large datasets in many different ways to spot patterns you might otherwise miss. Visualizations can also distill a dataset into an easy-to-grasp graph, map or chart to help readers quickly get the gist of a story. I've used data viz tools to help me see trends over time, which proved especially helpful for one story about pesticide use and another about violence in state psychiatric hospitals.

Among the many tools available for data visualization and analysis I've mostly used Tableau, which comes in both free (Tableau Public, https://public.tableau.com/en-us/s/) and commercial (Tableau Desktop, https://www.tableau.com) versions.

With Tableau Public, your visualizations are posted online, so anyone can see them, which isn't ideal for investigations in progress. But IRE members can request a free license to use both Tableau Desktop and a new tool called Tableau Prep, which helps you clean data before making visualizations. Tableau also offers free online training videos for both versions that provide an overview of the programs' features.

In addition to Tableau, there are numerous free tools to help you analyze and visualize datasets [7]. Visualization tools involve a bit of a learning curve, but most of them provide online tutorials to help you get up to speed fairly quickly. IRE offers hands-on workshops and trainings through boot camps and its annual Computer-Assisted Reporting Meeting (see Chapter 7 for more information). I also recommend the online tutorials offered by Buzzfeed's Peter Aldhous, peteraldhous.com/resources.html, who teaches data visualization at the Graduate School of Journalism at the University of California, Berkeley.

VERIFICATION CHECKLIST

Anything that makes it into your story needs to pass a series of questions: How do I know this? Why should the reader believe it? Am I presenting fact or innuendo? Are all of the charges I'm making supported by multiple sources I'm confident are telling the truth? Are they backed up by documents? Have I taken license with details to boost narrative drama that I can't defend as true? Have I committed sins of omission that could undercut the premise of the story? Have I anticipated criticisms and accounted for them in the story? Did I quote anyone out of context?

When I'm finished with a draft of a story, I vet each word in the piece using a technique I learned from fact-checkers at Parenting magazine, where I worked many years ago. I print out the draft and double-check every single thing that could be contested in the story — every fact, stated belief, quotation, assertion — and draw a line through it when I'm satisfied that it's true and I can show that it's true. I highlight in yellow anything that needs further corroboration. Then I confirm that the central premise of the story is supported and that any subjects of the investigation have been given a chance to respond. Views differ on when to contact a subject (for more on this, see Chapter 3), but in most cases, giving people several days to respond to an investigation that's taken weeks or months is reasonable.

Jayme Fraser, an investigative reporter with Oregon's Malheur Enterprise, takes a similar approach. At the end of an investigation, she prints out the story and goes through every sentence, highlighting facts, details or quotes in green and names in orange. Then she writes down the page of a document or interview that supports it.

Taking a systematic approach to getting the facts, and the context surrounding the facts, can help ensure that when you finally send your story out into the world, it's on solid ground. People or groups out to discredit your investigation as a "hit job" may do everything in their power to shoot holes in your story. You can of course correct any mistakes that come to your attention, but remember, they'll likely just be used by detractors to argue that your reporting can't be trusted. When you make the extra effort to bulletproof your story, readers will be able to see any blowback for what it is: not a good-faith effort to correct the record, but the PR spin of people trying to defend their reputations.

References

1. Philip Meyer, "The New Precision Journalism," 1991. https://www.unc.edu/~pmeyer/book/Chapter1.htm

2. Bill Kovach and Tom Rosenstiel, "The Elements of Journalism: What Newspeople Should Know and the Public Should Expect," Three Rivers Press, 2014.
3. Adeshina Emmanuel and Justin Ray, "Top Journalists Reveal the Best Reporting Advice They Have Received," Columbia Journalism Review, Aug. 14, 2017. https://www.cjr.org/special_report/margaret-sullivan-fahrenthold-ioffe-ben-smith-gay-talese-steve-coll.php
4. Hannah Hoag, "Liza Gross Digs into California's Pesticide Data," The Open Notebook, June 9, 2015. https://www.theopennotebook.com/2015/06/09/liza-gross-californias-pesticide-data/
5. Barry Yeoman, "The Inside Story of Shell's Arctic Assault," Audubon, Jan.-Feb. 2016. http://www.audubon.org/magazine/january-february-2016/the-inside-story-shells-arctic-assault
6. Charles Piller, "Called 'Hogwash,' a Gene Test for Addiction Risk Exploits Opioid Fears," STAT, Dec. 13, 2016. https://www.statnews.com/2016/12/13/proove-opioid-risk-test/
7. Sharon Machlis, "Chart and image gallery: 30+ free tools for data visualization and analysis," Computerworld, Aug. 1, 2016. https://www.computerworld.com/article/2506820/business-intelligence/business-intelligence-chart-and-image-gallery-30-free-tools-for-data-visualization-and-analysis.html

END NOTES

- ✓ With investigative stories, compared to explanatory stories, mistakes are more likely to be used to discredit your primary premise and reputation.
- ✓ Journalists can never be totally "objective," but systematic methods of verification can help you determine the objective validity of facts. Follow a system that allows you to gather and analyze facts in a transparent, reproducible way.
- ✓ Manage your biases by reporting against them. Look for information that could prove you wrong.
- ✓ Be prepared to reject your assumptions if you unearth information that contradicts them.
- ✓ Resist the urge to hype the drama with literary embellishments. They give your critics ammunition.
- ✓ Tell readers how you know what you know so they can decide for themselves whether it's credible.
- ✓ Provide links to the primary documents and data supporting your story if possible.
- ✓ Track documents, records requests, data, interviews and other key materials to stay organized over the course of an investigation.
- ✓ Annotate information and data analyses as you go to make fact-checking easier.
- ✓ Go through a draft of your story line by line to verify that every fact, and anything that could be contested, is true.

[6]

Investigative Ethics and Legal Issues

THE DRIVE TO EXPOSE WRONGDOING, fueled by a sense of outrage at injustice, motivates many a successful investigative reporter. That zeal can keep you focused on tedious tasks, like combing through hundreds of documents or analyzing thousands of rows of data. But it can also lead you into ethical gray zones and make you more susceptible to confirmation bias.

Confirmation bias is the tendency to interpret facts or evidence as support for beliefs or theories you already hold. When you believe you're unearthing critical, hidden information the public should know, you might be tempted to cut corners to overstate what your evidence indicates. Maybe multiple sources have told you "everybody knows" a scientist fabricates data and hides conflicts of interest to support a company you believe is causing harm. You don't have proof of your sources' allegations, but they fall in line with what you've long suspected. And you believe the scientist's behavior is helping the company harm public health, which the public has a right to know. You may not even realize you're beefing up evidence that bolsters the allegations while omitting details that don't.

Then there are intentional cases of deception, in which reporters make calculated decisions to practice subterfuge to reveal information of vital public interest that can't be obtained any other way — for example, using hidden cameras to expose police brutality or unsafe working conditions. Deception to obtain the truth is a highly controversial practice, and ethicists on both sides have provided journalists with in-depth considerations to ponder before practicing it. (See "Covert information gathering" below.)

Intentionally or not, though, when we misrepresent the truth, we mislead the public, and fail to uphold our ethical duty to the reader. But how can we guard against these deceptions if we don't even know we're committing them?

The verification tips laid out in Chapter 5 can keep your zeal in check to bolster the accuracy and credibility of your reporting, the foundation of ethical journalism. And though different ethical dilemmas arise with most every new investigation, you can also create a checklist to ensure that the decisions you make over the course of your reporting and writing are morally defensible. Start with the basic ethical principles that apply to all journalism: don't fabricate, don't steal copy and don't pay people to tell you things (although some argue there may be cases where this is justified).

Anyone who practices journalism, let alone investigative journalism, should be familiar with the Society of Professional Journalists' code of ethics. The SPJ code has long provided reporters with an ethical foundation, guided by four basic principles, most recently updated in 2014: Seek the truth and report it. Minimize harm. Act independently. Be accountable and transparent. Each principle is fleshed out, complete with position papers, on the SPJ website [1], to help journalists navigate the challenges and responsibilities involved in relaying information to the public.

In "The New Ethics of Journalism: Principles for the 21st Century" [2], editors Kelly McBride, media ethics expert and vice president of the Poynter Institute, and Tom Rosenstiel, executive director of the American Press Institute and co-author of "The Elements of Journalism," list three principles that "meld the core values of journalism with the democratic values of the digital era": Seek truth and report it as fully as possible. Be transparent. Engage community as an end, rather than as a means.

They argue that while independence is still important, in the new digital landscape, how journalism is produced is more important than who produces it. Transparency pulls back the curtain on the reporting process to show the public how journalism is produced, which they say will help drive intellectual honesty and integrity in journalists and so engage citizens. Embracing the idea that engaging citizens is critical to democracy in the digital age, they sought input from readers to help them adapt journalism's principles to contemporary needs.

"Journalism is an unlicensed profession, we don't have an ivory tower to set our ethics for us," McBride told me. "We have to turn to our users and ask, 'Is this working for you?'"

"When you talk to the users of journalism and ask them, 'What do you find helpful here?' one of the things they tell you is, 'It's really helpful when I understand why you are saying what you're saying, how you came to the decision to publish this information, and what your assumptions are that you brought to this work.'"

Show your work

Transparency not only reveals how you know what you know, it reveals the ethical choices you've made. If you're publishing a story that tarnishes a scientist's reputation by showing they've committed fraud or have a history of sexual harassment, readers should have enough information to appreciate why the story was published. Consider these questions:

- Did you provide evidence to support the charges?
- Have you violated the privacy of victims or potentially

caused them emotional distress?

- Is there a compelling reason to expose someone's private behaviors?
- Does the benefit to the public justify harm to the accused?

Following a robust process to verify your work helps you arrive at the best obtainable version of the truth. Once you arrive at that truth, give your readers enough information to follow your journey. Show them key materials that support whatever charges you're making by including links to your reporting materials whenever possible, though not to the point of distraction.

When I report on conflicts of interest or industry distortion of science, I try to provide links to the primary materials that support my story. If your investigation involves data analysis, note where you got the data and how you did the analysis. And if your outlet can support it, post the original spreadsheets. Ideally, your outlets should also post documents to Document Cloud (see Chapter 7), to avoid sending readers to bad links.

For a Verge story about the tobacco industry's covert influence on debates over the risks and benefits of vaping [3], I analyzed hundreds of internal tobacco company documents and scores of scientific papers. The tobacco documents revealed a longstanding industry strategy to get support for their "reduced harm" products by sowing divisions among public health experts. The industry documents, combined with court records, also showed that vaping advocates who claimed they had nothing to do with the tobacco industry had in fact relied on longtime industry allies and lawyers to fight their battles. The scientific papers pointed to a "funding effect," in which research sponsored by the industry tended to report that benefits from vaping outweighed potential risks, while independently funded research came to the opposite conclusion. The papers' conflicts of interest statements also helped me test suspicions that some particularly vocal promoters of vaping had ties to the industry.

I included links in the story to all the materials — scientific papers, court hearings and industry emails, grants and memos — that were critical to making my case. That way, readers could check the evidence I'd collected and decide for themselves whether it supported the main points in my story.

Explain What You Don't Know

Just as important as telling readers how you know what you know is telling them what you don't know. It was clear from internal company documents that the tobacco industry had planned to divide and conquer the tobacco control community by identifying moderates who might promote so-called safer cigarettes, while enlisting libertarian allies (whom they called "credible third parties") to denigrate moralistic "extremists" who wouldn't. I suspected that this strategy partly accounted for the polarized debate over e-cigarettes today, but I couldn't prove it, and said so. Instead, I showed that the same third parties that helped the tobacco industry promote "safer" cigarettes are using these old tactics to defend e-cigarettes today.

Come Up with Your Own Ethical Principles

If you muster the moral outrage to pursue an investigation, you'd best muster the moral responsibility to develop and follow a defensible code of ethics that helps you treat the material you gather, and the people in your story, in an even-handed manner. If you write a hard-hitting piece that charges someone with wrongdoing, your reputation is on the line too. You have to feel comfortable with what you're putting out there and what may happen as a result. The earlier you can think through the implications of what you're reporting, the more likely you'll be able to anticipate and address potential criticisms. Think about who beyond the principal subjects will be affected, and how you're going to feel if they attack what you've reported. Understand that no matter how fairly you've treated the subjects and issues under scrutiny, some people will criticize you for being unfair. If you're not comfortable with that, this type of story might not be for you.

Some of my stories have painted subjects in a bad light. I didn't feel good about it. For a story that ran in The Intercept about a sound science group [4], I wrestled with the question of whether the benefits of making some of the actors' actions public outweighed any negative impacts they might suffer. My editors and I ultimately decided that the public's right to know trumped concerns about the subjects' reputations.

There's no bright-line rule that applies to every situation. Each case is different. And different people are likely to come up with different answers to the same question. But I find that asking myself, "Is this issue something the public should know about?" keeps me focused on the reason I'm pursuing a given line of investigation in the first place.

Beyond that, I've come up with a set of general questions that guide my reporting:

- Have I considered alternative explanations for what I've found?
- Could there be anything I overlooked?
- Am I confident I got it right?
- How would I feel if the investigation were about me?
- Did I give subjects ample time and opportunity to respond to my key findings?

The particulars may vary, but creating and following a list of core values can help you avoid ethical lapses. In many ways, these principles echo those that guide you through the verification process, described in Chapter 5. That's because ethical and verification processes complement and reinforce each other.

If you work at a media outlet, chances are your organization has a protocol for dealing with ethical dilemmas. If you're a freelancer, and you're pretty sure where your story is likely to appear, find out what the publication's ethical standards are. If you have a commitment from an outlet, don't be shy about asking your editor for advice. Your editor should help you work through ethical issues in the reporting and writing, and help you come up with a process that guarantees the standards of the publication are being upheld. If you don't have an outlet lined up, you can also contact organizations like the Society of Professional Journalists and the Poynter Institute for advice (see Chapter 7).

Be honest in your reporting

In-person interviews are always preferable, but aren't always practical. If you interview someone on the phone and want to record the call, make sure you know your state's laws on recording without someone's knowledge. In California, it's illegal to record people without telling them. Other states allow it, but does that make it right? How would you feel if you found out someone had recorded your phone conversation without your knowledge? Imagine if a primary source found out you were recording and felt betrayed and decided to stop talking to you. Or they told other people you needed to speak with that you're not trustworthy.

If you're interviewing someone over the phone, don't assume the person expects you to record the call. Why take the risk that they'll view it as deceptive when you can easily mention it at the start of a call, as a general rule?

Treat subjects with respect

Confronting someone with information that makes them look bad can be unnerving. But remember that your ultimate loyalty is to the public, not to your sources. I tell myself that the public's right to know outweighs my squeamishness about asking someone to explain their questionable actions or unsavory behavior (see Chapter 3 for more on confronting sources).

Sometimes a subject of an investigation can inadvertently offer incriminating evidence. One person I interviewed for a story on tobacco industry influence over the vaping debate yelled at me for most of the hour we talked on the phone. I told him my reporting showed that he signed on to a brief to fight e-cigarette regulations with a law firm that had a history of helping the tobacco industry using similar arguments to evade regulations and defeat smokers' liability claims. When I tried to ask him about working with a tobacco industry law firm, he cut me off, and said he was surprised I'd read the brief — and then told me he'd come up with that strategy. I hadn't expected him to admit that, but he seemed to view it as an accomplishment.

Be sure to tell a person everything you've discovered about them, and don't cut corners. If a source denies something in the story after it runs, and you discover you got it wrong, correct the mistake. If it turns out you're right, share your notes or segment of the recording with the source. If they insist you misunderstood what they said, set up a time to talk to resolve the discrepancy, even though the story's already been published.

You also need to give the person enough time to respond to the charges before publication. When the online outlet Babe ran a story accusing Aziz Ansari of sexual misconduct based on one anonymous source, it gave him barely five hours to comment before the story ran, according to The Guardian.

Ansari is a comedian, but the same rules apply for coverage of sexual misconduct among scientists. Is five hours a reasonable amount of time to give someone a chance to respond to a charge that could ruin their career? Would it be for you, if you were accused?

COVERT INFORMATION GATHERING

Going undercover for exposés dates back to early muckrakers like Upton Sinclair, who blended in with meatpackers to reveal inhumane conditions suffered by workers and livestock in the industry. More recently Shane Bauer spent four months undercover as a prison guard for Mother Jones. Other undercover practices include using hidden cameras or existing surveillance videos to expose abuse or corruption.

Ethics experts continue to debate whether such covert practices are ever warranted. Some contend they're never justified because they subvert the journalist's obligation to tell the truth, while others argue they can be when the reporting produces highly significant public benefits. (For in-depth resources on ethics, see Chapter 7.)

"The Investigative Reporter's Handbook" [5], published by IRE, says journalists considering going undercover should ask themselves:

- Is it possible to get evidence from other sources?
- Will undercover work substantially boost the story's accuracy and credibility?
- Will the reported results be important and alarming enough to overshadow the deceptive practices?

For Poynter's McBride, acts of deception demand extraordinary circumstances: "I think you have to have exhausted every other way of getting information, and the target of your investigation has to be so critically important."

LET YOUR EDITOR CHALLENGE YOU

When you've been reporting on a topic for weeks (or longer), you may get lulled into a false sense of security that the assumptions you're making and the narrative you're creating are true, and that anyone who doesn't see that just doesn't know the material well enough. But this is a dangerous frame of mind. If your editor challenges something you're saying, especially your main thesis, don't get defensive. Keep an open mind and listen carefully to their questions. Good editors will rein in your zeal, and hubris, and challenge your assumptions. They'll ask you if you've considered other explanations and, if so, why you rejected them in favor of the one you're pursuing.

FACT-CHECKERS ARE YOUR FRIENDS

Pretty much anyone who makes a living as a journalist has suffered the pangs of having to issue a correction. Corrections are maddening, but we correct the record as soon as we can and move on. Corrections in an investigative story, for even the most minor error, can be used to cast doubt on the credibility of your central premise and undercut weeks or months of work. But it's far less damaging to cop to the error yourself than have it disclosed by others, especially the targets of an investigation.

Fact-checkers are there to make sure that doesn't happen. They retrace the steps you took to reach your conclusions by reviewing your primary documents, contacting your sources and verifying every statement of fact, and even quoted opinions, in your story. It's your responsibility to get everything right, but they're your safety net. They're likely to catch inconsistencies or errors you can't see anymore because you're so deep in the weeds of your investigation.

I've heard fact-checkers vent about reporters who get angry when their assumptions are questioned. But that type of attitude is self-destructive. Fact-checkers help ensure the story you're telling is true. Treat them with respect and try to make their job easier. Annotate all your facts as you collect them, organize your materials and note where you obtained data and documents to help them help you.

GUARD AGAINST CONFLICTS OF INTERESTS

If you're doing investigative reporting, it's especially important to guard against any real or perceived competing interests that could be construed as biasing your reporting. This can be harder for freelancers who need to diversify their assignments to make a living. Still, it's important to ask yourself how a given activity might look to outsiders so you can determine whether your choice of assignment could pose a conflict of interest. Do you do public relations for an environmental organization? You can't do a story that accuses a company of polluting a river without expecting the company's defenders to discredit you as an environmental activist. Have you worked with a nonprofit funded by the organic food industry? Don't think you can write about Monsanto in a negative light without facing the wrath of a well-oiled biotech product defense machine.

You can also steer clear of conflicts of interest by following these basic don'ts:

- Don't get too close to your sources.
- Don't accept money or gifts from sources.
- Don't donate to political campaigns or advocacy groups or activities, even if you don't cover them.
- Don't sign petitions in the areas you cover.
- Don't buy stock in companies you might potentially cover.
- Don't accept paid travel junkets from sources.

Of course, plenty of gray areas are likely to crop up, though common sense can help you decide whether something could conceivably be seen as compromising your ability to report fairly and accurately. Ask yourself how you would feel if the potential conflict came to light after the story ran. Would you be embarrassed? Could you explain that it had no impact on the choice of subject or outcome of the investigation? As always, when in doubt, consult with your editor.

GET TO KNOW MEDIA LAW

The fear of getting sued can keep even the best investigative reporters up at night. Anyone considering an investigative project should have a copy of the Associated Press Briefing on Media Law on hand [6]. The briefing outlines the laws governing access to government information, how you gather news, how you treat confidential sources, defamation (which in both print and broadcast journalism typically means libel), privacy and copyright infringement. Once your story is published, you can get in legal hot water if it contains errors that harm someone's reputation, contains *accurate* information but violates someone's right to privacy or includes material that infringes on someone's copyright.

If you portray someone who is not a public figure in a "false light" — by embellishing or distorting details about a person in a way that gives a misleading impression — you could be liable for invasion of privacy. (False light doesn't require that a statement be defamatory, just false.)

It's beyond the scope of this handbook to explore these laws, but it's a good idea to have a grasp of the ways a story could put you in legal jeopardy. And if you're doing investigative reporting as a freelancer, even if you're only adding investigative elements to a story, you absolutely must understand the risks you face as an individual. It's important to remember that nailing down every last detail is no guarantee you won't be sued by someone who claims you've damaged their reputation.

That's what happened to Amy Wallace, a freelancer who wrote a profile for Wired of Dr. Paul Offit, a pediatrician, co-inventor of the rotavirus vaccine and favorite target of anti-vaccine activists for his outspoken advocacy of childhood vaccines. In her story, which ran online as "An Epidemic of Fear: How Panicked Parents Skipping Shots Endanger Us All" [7], Wallace also profiled people who believe vaccines cause autism and pose other risks to children.

Two months after the story ran, Wallace was served with a notice informing her that she was being sued (along with Offit and Condé Nast, which publishes Wired) for $1 million. Barbara Loe Fisher, co-founder and head of the anti-vaccine National Vaccine Information Center, objected to a quote of Offit's in the piece — "She lies," he said, referring to Fisher's tactics to rally others against him.

Wallace wrote about the hair-raising experience of being sued for the Center for Health Journalism's blog [8]. Fisher had alleged that the quote "constituted a false statement of fact about her that would cause people to conclude that she is not a person of honesty or integrity," Wallace wrote. "In this way, she alleged, I (along with Dr. Offit, and Condé Nast) had defamed her and caused her to appear 'odious, infamous and ridiculous.'"

The suit was dismissed. "But not before thousands of hours (and countless dollars) were spent proving how fair the story was," Wallace wrote.

I was also threatened with a lawsuit when I wrote about the forces perpetuating the myth that vaccines cause autism for PLOS Biology [9]. The people who alleged I'd defamed them and harmed their daughter — by reporting, accurately, that they'd claimed in court documents and publicly that she was injured by vaccines — eventually backed down. Luckily I was on staff, so would not have been on the hook for legal fees. But it still took hours and hours of work to counter the claims and attest to the story's fairness.

Though neither of these stories was investigative in the traditional sense, they do illustrate a risk inherent in investigative reporting: blowback from those you're holding accountable. A person claiming defamation has to prove the objectionable statements are false. But as the cases above demonstrate, you can get it right and still get sued.

Questions around what constitutes invasion of privacy and

copyright infringement can be tricky, but Reporters Committee for Freedom of the Press offers resources on both to help you think through the issues, as well as a legal hotline if you need immediate advice [10].

DON'T SIGN THE INDEMNITY CLAUSE

When you do freelance investigative reporting, it's critical to understand that many media outlets' contracts place the responsibility for libel, plagiarism and other legal claims on the writer, rather than on the outlet running the story. They typically do this by adding a clause that states in one way or another that the writer indemnifies the publisher against any liability, cost or expense incurred as a result of the work — meaning you're responsible for any legal claims related to the work. Simply put, you won't stay in business long if you sign contracts that hold you legally responsible if a subject of your investigation sues for defamation, invasion of privacy or copyright infringement. If the outlet won't change contract text that leaves you liable, insist on a written agreement that says their legal staff will represent you in the event of a lawsuit, frivolous or not.

FIND PARTNERS THAT SHIELD YOU FROM LIABILITY

Some organizations act as an intermediary between journalists and media outlets and assume legal liability for the freelancers who belong to their networks. The Food and Environment Reporting Network, for example, not only shields the freelancers they work with but enlists lawyers to review controversial stories for any legal red flags.

When I wrote a story for The Intercept about a so-called sound science group that had a long history of promoting shady evidence to defend corporate interests, FERN's legal team reviewed the story, even though it had already gone through legal review at The

Intercept. Neither review found anything worrisome, but having the extra support from FERN helped provide an extra layer of assurance that the story was on solid legal footing. It also helped me sleep better at night. And since not all media outlets provide legal review, FERN can give freelancers the type of legal support that staffers enjoy.

References

1. Society of Professional Journalists' Code of Ethics. https://www.spj.org/ethicscode.asp
2. Kelly McBride and Tom Rosenstiel (eds.), "The New Ethics of Journalism: Principles for the 21st Century," CQ Press, 2014.
3. Liza Gross, "Smoke Screen," The Verge, Nov. 16, 2017. https://www.theverge.com/2017/11/16/16658358/vape-lobby-vaping-health-risks-nicotine-big-tobacco-marketing
4. Liza Gross, "Seeding Doubt: How Self-Appointed Guardians of 'Sound Science' Tip the Scales Toward Industry," The Intercept, Nov. 15, 2016. https://theintercept.com/2016/11/15/how-self-appointed-guardians-of-sound-science-tip-the-scales-toward-industry/
5. Brant Houston and Investigative Reporters and Editors, Inc., "The Investigative Reporter's Handbook: A Guide to Documents, Databases and Techniques, 5th Edition," Bedford/St. Martin's. 2009.
6. Associated Press, "The Associated Press Stylebook and Briefing on Media Law," Basic Books, 2018.

7. Amy Wallace, "An Epidemic of Fear: How Panicked Parents Skipping Shots Endanger Us All," Wired, Oct. 19, 2009. https://www.wired.com/2009/10/ff_waronscience/
8. Amy Wallace, "Covering Vaccines: Science, Policy and Politics in the Minefield," Center for Health Journalism blog. https://www.centerforhealthjournalism.org/resources/lessons/covering-vaccines
9. Liza Gross, "A Broken Trust: Lessons from the Vaccine-Autism Wars," PLoS Biology, May 26, 2009. http://journals.plos.org/plosbiology/article?id=10.1371/journal.pbio.1000114
10. Reporters Committee for Freedom of the Press. https://www.rcfp.org/legal-hotline

END NOTES

- ✓ Accuracy is a critical element of ethical journalism. Create a checklist to ensure that your reporting decisions guard against confirmation bias and are morally defensible.
- ✓ Showing readers how you know what you're telling them reveals your ethical choices too, and allows them to judge whether the public good is served by revealing damaging information about someone.
- ✓ Provide links to primary materials that support your key points.
- ✓ Remember: when you charge someone with wrongdoing, your reputation is on the line too. Ask yourself if the benefits of making a person's actions public outweigh potential consequences to the subject.
- ✓ Check your state's laws on recording conversations and consider the consequences of not letting a source know that you're recording, even if it's legal to do so.
- ✓ Fact-checkers are your safety net. Annotate your stories carefully to let them help you.
- ✓ Read primers on media law to understand the ways a story could put you in legal jeopardy.
- ✓ Carefully read freelance contracts. Don't let outlets hold you responsible for legal claims.

[7]

Funding, Resources and Further Reading

IN THE PREVIOUS CHAPTERS, I've drawn on lessons from my own experience, from numerous books, essays and tip sheets written by veteran investigators and, especially, from the wisdom of the many accomplished investigative reporters and journalists who've taught and inspired me over the years. Below, you'll find resources to help you delve more deeply into the issues covered in this handbook, as well as organizations that provide financial, logistical and legal support to investigative reporters.

Funding

Earth Journalism Network Biodiversity Media Initiative

Earth Journalism Network, in partnership with Arcadia (a charitable fund that supports cultural heritage and the environment), offers awards of $1,000 to $2,000 through the Biodiversity Story Fund to support investigative reporting that uses innovative approaches to storytelling. Priority is given to proposals that focus on areas with high species diversity, such as the Amazon, Central Africa and Southeast Asia, and applicants proposing to conduct investigative or enterprise reporting on these topics.
http://earthjournalism.net/projects/biodiversity-story-fund

Fund for Environmental Journalism

This fund from the Society of Environmental Journalists awards grants of up to $5,000 twice annually to support environmental reporting projects and entrepreneurial ventures. The fund also supports the Lizzie Grossman Grant for Environmental Health Reporting (named for the late environmental health reporter and SEJ member Elizabeth Grossman), which awards up to $5,000 to underwrite travel and other expenses related to a series of articles or other sustained coverage on an environmental health topic.
https://www.sej.org/initiatives/fund-for-environmental-journalism

Fund for Investigative Journalism

This grant (up to $10,000) gives priority to stories that "break new ground and expose wrongdoing — such as corruption, malfeasance, or misuse of power — in the public and private sectors." Grants cover out-of-pocket expenses (travel, document collection and equipment rental) and considers requests for small stipends.
http://fij.org/

The International Women's Media Foundation Howard G. Buffett Fund for Women Journalists

Supports "ambitious projects and underreported, globally important stories." The IWMF notes that it will award an annual total of $230,000 worth of grants for the next eight years to support women journalists, and that the fund is not limited in either the grant dollar amount or the number of grants awarded each year.
https://www.iwmf.org/programs/howard-g-buffett-fund-for-women-journalists/

The Investigative Fund at The Nation Institute

Sponsored by The Nation, this fund awards $500 to $10,000 for investigative projects, including the twice-annual I.F. Stone Award. Priority is given to "highly original reporting on important stories with the potential to have social impact."
https://www.theinvestigativefund.org/about/faq/

IRE Freelance Fellowship

IRE awards $1,000 or more to journalists who make their living primarily as freelancers. A three-judge panel reviews proposals partly on the breadth, significance and potential impact of the project. The fellowship donor asks that priority be given to proposals dealing with whistleblowers, business ethics and/or privacy issues, though other topics will be seriously considered.
https://ire.org/events-and-training/fellowships-and-scholarships/freelance-fellowship/

Leonard C. Goodman Institute for Investigative Reporting

Provides editorial and financial support to journalists "pursuing in-depth investigative projects that align with In These Times' mission of advancing democracy and economic justice, informing movements for a more humane world and providing an accessible forum for debate about the policies that shape our future." Grantees are published in In These Times, compensated for travel and other expenses and paid a "competitive per-word rate."
http://inthesetimes.com/investigative

The Pulitzer Center on Crisis Reporting

Awards grants of $5,000 to $15,000 (sometimes higher) to support international travel costs associated with reporting projects "on topics and regions of global importance, with an emphasis on

issues that have gone unreported or underreported in the mainstream American media."
http://pulitzercenter.org/grants#travelgrants

The Reporting Award

Offered annually by the Arthur L. Carter Journalism Institute of New York University, the award provides grants up to $12,500 for "a work of journalism in any medium on significant underreported subjects in the public interest." In establishing the award, the institute's faculty cited "the need for encouraging enterprise journalism during a time of extensive layoffs and budget cuts throughout the journalism industry."
https://journalism.nyu.edu/about-us/awards-and-fellowships/the-reporting-award/

The Science [magazine] Fund for Investigative Reporting

Science magazine funds ambitious projects in investigative reporting and data journalism to "tell stories about the scientific community and its practices, the influence of money and politics in science and science-related public policy that can only be brought to light through extensive reporting, documents and data."
http://www.sciencemag.org/news/investigative-journalism-fund

ORGANIZATIONS THAT SUPPORT INVESTIGATIVE REPORTERS

Association of Health Care Journalists

A nonprofit organization that works to promote the quality, accumracy and visibility of health care reporting, writing and editing, and offers in-depth tip sheets on accessing data to investigate health.
https://healthjournalism.org/

Food and Environment Reporting Network

FERN commissions and provides in-depth investigative and explanatory stories as well as editorial, financial and at times legal support to reporters and partners with print, broadcast and online outlets. FERN occasionally pays reporters to research a story idea to see if it might justify a full project.
https://thefern.org/report-for-us/

Freelance Investigative Reporters and Editors

A collaboration between IRE and Project Word, which supports freelance investigative reporting with financial support from IRE. FIRE helps investigative freelancers place their work in various media outlets and offers two services: The Editorial Consultancy provides up to an hour of help, on a one-time basis (for example, editorial feedback, funding tips and referrals for independent reporters) and The Virtual Newsroom provides in-depth services to freelancers that newsrooms traditionally provide, such as research assistance, legal review, professional trainings and access to freelance editors, and occasionally stipends.
http://projectword.org/fire/about

Global Investigative Journalism Network

This international association of nonprofit organizations supports, promotes and produces investigative journalism, runs trainings, sponsors conferences and provides resources and consulting to investigative journalists around the world.
https://gijn.org/

Media Helping Media

Offers free online training resources, including modules on investigative reporting.
http://www.mediahelpingmedia.org/

National Association of Science Writers

NASW does not offer grants specifically for investigative reporting, but has funded investigative projects, such as this handbook, through the Peggy Girshman Idea Grant.
https://www.nasw.org/article/about-peggy-girshman-idea-grants

New England Center for Investigative Reporting

NECIR produces and teaches "in-depth journalism with impact" and offers training to high school students through the Pre-College Summer Journalism Institute at Boston University.
http://studentprograms.necir.org/

Society of Environmental Journalists

Nonprofit organization for journalists covering the environment offers watchdog tip sheets and other resources to facilitate investigative reporting on the environment.
www.sej.org

FACT-CHECKING AND INVESTIGATIVE REPORTING GUIDES

The Chicago Guide to Fact-Checking, by Brooke Borel.
Offers an in-depth look at the nuts and bolts of getting it right, to maintain your credibility and readers' trust.

The Elements of Journalism, What Newspeople Should Know and the Public Should Expect, by Bill Kovach and Tom Rosenstiel.
Updates the classic book on journalism's critical relationship to democracy, with an in-depth chapter on verification.

The Fact-Checker's Bible: A Guide to Getting It Right, by Sarah Harrison Smith.
Covers everything from ensuring accuracy to plagiarism and legal

liability, based on her experience as fact checker at The New Yorker and The New York Times Magazine.

From the Experts: Tips and Tools for Investigations
The Global Investigative Journalism Network's YouTube channel features videos on effective use of data, understanding public documents, managing investigations and much more.
http://bit.ly/2jum1XS

How to Become a Mouthpiece for the People
An electronic manual on investigative journalism published by the Konrad-Adenauer-Stiftung Media Programme Asia.
http://www.investigative-manual.org/wp-content/uploads/2016/09/20171026-IJM_final.pdf

Investigative Journalism, Proven Strategies for Reporting the Story, by William C. Gaines.
Immerses writers in the mindset, techniques and ethical dilemmas of investigative reporters through real-life examples, including cautionary tales and advice on "how not to do it."

The Investigative Reporter's Handbook, A Guide to Documents, Databases and Techniques, by Brant Houston and Investigative Reporters and Editors, Inc.
The investigative reporter's bible. Provides a comprehensive guide to the resources and techniques reporters need to plan and execute investigations.

Investigative Reporting, Advanced Techniques and Methods, by John Ullmann.
Offers advice on surmounting barriers to doing investigations, honing detective skills and finding and producing better projects.

The New Precision Journalism, A Reporter's Introduction to Social Science Methods, by Philip Meyer.
Introduces reporters to social science research techniques to enhance the depth and accuracy of stories.

Story-Based Inquiry, A Manual for Investigative Journalists, by Mark Lee Hunter, et al., UNESCO.
This free manual, based on a combination of academic research and decades' worth of experience from experts at the Global Investigative Journalism Network, walks reporters through the basics of conceiving, structuring, researching, composing and publishing an investigation.
http://www.storybasedinquiry.com/

Working with Whistleblowers, A Guide for Journalists, produced by the Government Accountability Project.
http://www.whistleblower.org/sites/default/files/whistleblowerguide.pdf

COMPUTER-ASSISTED REPORTING RESOURCES

CAR boot camps
Sponsored by IRE, these in-depth workshops introduce reporters to methods of acquiring and analyzing data, using database managers and mining data to tell compelling stories.
https://www.ire.org/events-and-training/boot-camps/

Document Cloud
A tool founded "on the belief that if journalists were more open about their sourcing, the public would be more inclined to trust their reporting." The tool helps journalists share, analyze, annotate and publish source documents to the open web.

FollowTheMoney.org
This database, operated by the nonpartisan, nonprofit National Institute on Money in State Politics, includes campaign-donor, lobbyist and other information from government disclosure agencies nationwide. Data are downloadable and freely available.
https://www.followthemoney.org/

Industry Documents Library
A portal to millions of documents, many previously secret communications released through litigation, created by industries that influence public health, run by the UCSF Library and Center for Knowledge Management.
https://www.industrydocumentslibrary.ucsf.edu/

Journalism Ethics: A Casebook of Professional Conduct for News Media, by Fred Brown and other SPJ members.
Examines 50 case studies and legal implications to promote ethical thinking in journalism.

National Institute of Computer-Assisted Reporting
An IRE program that trains journalists in accessing and analyzing digital information and holds an annual conference that features intensive hands-on trainings.
https://www.ire.org/nicar/

OpenCorporates
An openly licensed database listing an ever-expanding list of companies around the world.
https://opencorporates.com

Open Payments

A federal program, required by the Affordable Care Act, that collects information about payments drug and device companies make to physicians and teaching hospitals for travel, research, gifts, speaking fees and meals.
https://www.cms.gov/openpayments

PACER (Public Access to Court Electronic Records).
Provides online access to U.S. appellate, district and bankruptcy court records and documents nationwide.
https://www.pacer.gov/

Project Toxicdocs

A database of millions of freely available, previously confidential documents on industrial poisons curated by Columbia University and the City University of New York.
https:// www.toxicdocs.org/

Tools for Extracting Data and Text from PDFs

A list of tools and services for scraping PDFs with a focus on free open source options, compiled by Open Knowledge Labs.
http://okfnlabs.org/blog/2016/04/19/pdf-tools-extract-text-and-data-from-pdfs.html

Watchdog workshops

These workshops, led by IRE staff and local journalists, are held in cities around the country each year. They're designed to help reporters find key documents and data to add depth to regular stories and produce quick-hit enterprise stories. Most workshops also offer tips on bulletproofing stories and digging deeper using search engines.
https://www.ire.org/events-and-training/watchdog-workshops/

FOIA, ETHICAL, LEGAL AND OTHER RESOURCES

Digital Security for Journalists

Journalist's Resource (an online database curated by Harvard's Shorenstein Center on Media, Politics and Public Policy) offers tips on protecting your sources and yourself.
https://journalistsresource.org/tip-sheets/reporting/digital-security-tips-protecting-sources-journalist

FOIA Advocates

A project of FOIA attorneys David Bahr and Daniel Stotter designed to assist the public in gaining access to records from federal, state and local governments using FOIA, state and local public records laws.
http://www.foiadvocates.com/records.html

FOIA Mapper

A centralized, searchable catalog of government records created by independent data journalist Max Galka with support from the Knight Foundation.
https://foiamapper.com/

The FOIA Project

A collaboration of academic and media organizations that tracks cases in which the federal government grants or withholds records under the Freedom of Information Act.
http://foiaproject.org/about/

Journalists Toolbox

Comprehensive online resource run by the Society of Professional Journalists that offers courses and tips on First Amendment rights, FOIA, digital security, ethics, fact-checking and more.
https://www.journaliststoolbox.org/

Media Hacks
Provides resources and tips on digital and data reporting, run by journalists.
http://mediahack.co.za/

New York Times Ethical Journalism: A Handbook of Values and Practices for the News and Editorial Departments
This guide helps reporters cover news "without fear or favor" and to treat readers, news sources, advertisers and others fairly and openly.
https://www.nytimes.com/editorial-standards/ethical-journalism.html

Poynter Institute
Offers trainings and resources in ethics, fact-checking, managing investigations and more. https:// www.poynter.org/. See also 10 questions journalists should ask to help them make ethical decisions from Bob Steele, the Poynter Institute's Nelson Poynter Scholar for Journalism Values:
https://www.poynter.org/news/ask-these-10-questions-make-good-ethical-decisions.

Public Records Generator
A tool designed by the Student Press Law Center to help journalists request access to records held by state or local government agencies or entities (for example, public school districts, city or campus police departments or state boards of health).
http://www.splc.org/page/lettergenerator

Reporters Committee for Freedom of the Press
Provides in-depth resources and advice to reporters on issues, including state and federal open government laws, access to

electronic records, libel laws, reporters' shield laws around the country, access to court documents and proceedings and more. Maintains a 24-hour emergency Legal Defense and FOIA Hotline, 1-800-336-4243.
http://www.rcfp.org

The Society of Professional Journalists
Provides a FOIA toolkit (https://www.spj.org/foi-guide-pros.asp) and a Legal Defense Fund (https://www.spj.org/ldf.asp) to support litigation to ensure public access to government records and proceedings. Also see SPJ's Code of Ethics:
https://www.spj.org/ethicscode.asp

The Whistleblower Project
A collaboration of the Society of Professional Journalists and the Government Accountability Project and other whistleblowing and media organizations, the project educates journalists on best practices to work safely with whistleblowers.
https://www.spj.org/whistleblower/

Afterword

THE IDEA FOR THIS HANDBOOK emerged from countless conversations with science writers who wanted to try investigative reporting but didn't know where to start. The conversations often began with questions about how I got into investigative reporting. I would usually respond with some variation on, "It's complicated."

My interest in investigative reporting followed naturally from my desire to understand unequal power dynamics and the conditions that lead to social inequality, environmental destruction and disease. I launched my first investigative project, which also happened to be my first big science story, nearly 20 years ago at Sierra magazine. I had scant experience doing either type of reporting, but resolved to pick up the skills I needed along the way.

The story, "Cancer, Inc.," grew out of my frustration with feel-good breast cancer awareness campaigns that pushed early detection as "your best protection" against the disease. Aside from being illogical — if you're detecting cancer, it's too late to prevent it — the messages, repeated ad nauseam, drowned out calls to regulate cancer-causing chemicals. This Orwellian message made more sense once I discovered that chemical manufacturers sponsored the "awareness" campaigns. And this discovery, combined with a healthy dose of outrage, inspired an intensive investigation (co-written with Sharon Batt, now an adjunct professor in the Department of Bioethics at Dalhousie University in Halifax, Nova Scotia) that revealed a deeply conflicted web of interests between the chemical and chemotherapy industries, which backed nationwide campaigns to shift discussions about cancer prevention to detection and treatment.

Not surprisingly, I picked up considerable knowledge and skills while investigating the story. After a brief stint at a science museum, I continued to do occasional investigative projects, with the help of tip sheets, generous advice from veteran investigators and sheer determination. My investigations followed my interests (and, in some cases, my obsessions). In one story, I showed how the U.S. Fish and Wildlife Service under President George W. Bush used dubious science to allow unbridled development in the Florida panther's already insufficient habitat, placing this critically endangered species at even greater risk. In another, I uncovered hidden industry campaigns that not only cast doubt on evidence about the health risks of the ubiquitous synthetic chemical bisphenol A but also attacked the scientists who'd discovered the risks. And in a story that unleashed a torrent of hate mail — and helped me grow a thicker skin — I explored the networks of anti-vaccination activists who distorted science to peddle long-rejected theories that vaccines cause autism, scaring worried parents and fueling the resurgence of vaccine-preventable diseases.

Finally, in 2011, more than a decade after my first investigative story, I sought formal training in investigative reporting. That's when I discovered the program (now offered to students) at the New England Center for Investigative Reporting, and met Joe Bergantino. He and NECIR co-founder Maggie Mulvihill immersed reporters in the tools, techniques, ethics and mindset of investigative reporting. I'd gone to the training hoping to come up with a reporting plan for a story about California legislators' failure to regulate flame retardants, in spite of mounting evidence of the chemicals' harm. Joe and Maggie helped me focus my primary question and come up with a reporting strategy. Six months later, my investigation, "Money to Burn" — which documented a $23 million chemical-industry campaign to wine and dine legislators and block five flame retardant bills — ran in Environmental Health News and was syndicated in several California weeklies.

The NECIR training gave me the foundation I needed to investigate a wide range of topics, and the confidence to attempt even more ambitious projects. It also crystallized much of what I'd learned on the fly over the years. It turns out that I had learned a considerable amount about how to do investigative reporting simply by doing it. And that's a lesson that bears repeating. As Charles Piller told me, "If you want to do this work you've just got to do it. You've got to get started and build a reputation for yourself in the fields of your interest, and then ride that to the next story and the next."

Thinking back to the conversations I had with colleagues about investigative reporting, I remember being surprised that many highly accomplished science writers had avoided investigative reporting not because they had no interest in it, but because they found it mysterious and intimidating. These conversations seemed to put the lie to the oft-repeated trope that science writers are just interested in the wonder of nature and don't care about holding powerful people accountable.

Curious science writers have a knack for finding compelling stories about science. I hope this handbook gives any writer who's ever thought about investigative reporting the skills and confidence to follow their interests, and outrage, to do the digging that reveals the deeper stories behind those stories.

ACKNOWLEDGMENTS

Thanks to the National Association of Science Writers' executive board, officers, staff and grants committee for the Peggy Girshman Idea Grant that made this project possible. Thanks as well to NASW Executive Director Tinsley Davis for her patience, support and encouragement throughout the production of this handbook.

I'm grateful to the members of SciLance, who encouraged me to pursue this project, particularly to Michelle Nijhuis, Anne Sasso, Sarah Webb and Kendall Powell for advice on funding; to Susan Moran for moral support; to Hannah Hoag for her perceptive copy editing and to Thomas Hayden for graciously providing a safety net. I'm also grateful to Betsy Mason, Lynne Friedmann and many other colleagues for their enthusiastic support and belief that this handbook could inspire others to launch their own investigations.

Special thanks to Deborah Blum, Valerie Brown, Sharon Lerner, Kelly McBride, Charles Piller, John Upton and Barry Yeoman for sharing their experiences and tips. Thanks also to Paul Overberg and especially to Cheryl Phillips for sharing their considerable insights into the investigative reporting mindset and process and to Jacqui Banaszynski for showing me how to make readers care. I owe a special debt of gratitude to Joe Bergantino for reading and commenting on a draft of this handbook, having already taught me the essentials of investigative reporting.

Eternal thanks to Barry Bergman, my first reader (always), sounding board and partner.

INDEX

ABOUT THE AUTHOR

Liza Gross is an independent journalist whose investigative reporting has appeared in The Nation, The Intercept, Reveal (from the Center for Investigative Reporting), The Verge and other outlets, and who has written freelance stories for The New York Times and The Washington Post. She's also a contributor to "The Science Writers' Handbook" and a reporter for the Food and Environment Reporting Network, an independent, nonprofit news organization that produces award-winning, high-impact investigative and explanatory reporting on food, agriculture and environmental health. Her investigations — which have examined issues including unchecked violence in psychiatric hospitals, industry bias in "sound science" groups, government failures to protect Latino children from pesticides and vaping advocates' hidden ties to the tobacco industry — have received national awards and recognition in the 2016 "Best American Science and Nature Writing" anthology. She lives in the San Francisco Bay Area with her husband and two cats.

Printed in Great Britain
by Amazon